SCENTED BOO

The Flavours and Scents of Italy

TRADITIONAL ITALIAN CUISINE: RECIPES AND RESTAURANTS

L'ORTENSIA ROSSA

L'ORTENSIA ROSSA SRL (GRUPPO LOZZI EDITORI SINCE 1935)
Circ. Gianicolense 210 - 00152 Rome • Tel.: 06.98387080-1-2-3 • Fax: 06 5349779
E-mail: info@ortensiarossa.it

GRAPHIC DESIGN AND LAYOUT: Line Art Studio (Rome)
TEXT: Silvia Guglielmi
EDITED BY: Francesca Faramondi, Laura Cavallo

QUADERNI DELL'ORTENSIA ROSSA (I) - ISSN 2035-9578 - Monthly Periodical
Registrazione Tribunale di Roma n. 18/2009 del 16/01/2009

Registered Court of Rome n. 18/2009 on 16 January 2009
Managing Director: Silvia Guglielmi
Printed in the month of July at: MB STAMPA S.R.L. (Ariccia)

INTRODUCTION

Flipping through these pages you will find tempting photos and recipes to inspire you to try an incredible variety of traditional Italian specialties. Anyone who loves to cook will enjoy trying out the various cooking styles and discovering all the differences. This culinary atlas is in your hands: it is up to you to choose the pathway to discover new flavours and ancient pleasures.

THE RECIPES

- *The recipes are divided by region and by courses in the following order: APPETIZERS, FIRST COURSES, SECOND COURSES, SIDE DISHES AND DESSERTS (not all courses are included for each region)*
- *The quantities indicated make 4 servings*
- *In most cases the ingredients are easy to find. Alternatives are suggested for ingredients that are less common.*

TRADITIONAL PRODUCTS

The recipes have been paired with regional products that highlight a patrimony of wine and food specialties loved worldwide.

TRADITIONAL RESTAURANTS

Selected restaurants that serve the specialties illustrated here are listed for each region. The restaurants are all located in regional capitals.

Regional Index

Regional Index

ABRUZZO

The flavour of these untamed lands in the Apennine Mountains is reflected in some of the ingredients used in the local cuisine and a special place of honour is reserved for saffron. The local variety of this specialty is the most expensive in the world. It all began several centuries ago when a monk decided to see if it was possible to grow saffron here. The venture was an absolute success and today the famous crocus is the absolute pride of the Navelli zone in the Aquila Province. The price may seem high, but you should consider that one kilo of saffron requires over one hundred thousand flowers – that must be gathered by hand at dawn! In Navelli saffron is combined with chickpeas – another local specialty – at a festival held during the second half of August. At the opposite end of the scale we find a more commonly used condiment: hot pepper – widely appreciated for its ability to preserve foods as well. In Abruzzo, this condiment is very common and goes by a number of names including Diavolillo, lazzarillo, cazzariello, saittì and pepentò.

Abruzzo has fine meats and is known for lamb or goat specialties and its incredible cheeses (caciocavallo, ricotta and scamorza...). There are a number of local pork specialties including liver sausage (spicy hot pepper or honey sweet cured), the incredible Mortadellina di Campotosto (a small lean lightly smoked salami with bits of seasoned lard at the centre) and Ventricina from the Vasto area (with lots of hot pepper).

Another important resource is beans. The crop grows well here and beyond the chick peas mentioned above, fava beans are another popular variety used dry in a number of recipes and the local variety of lentils is one of the best (small size and tender skin). They compare with the famous lentils of Castelluccio and can be prepared in a thousand different ways from the first course to the dessert course. The mountains end at the sea which provides the local cuisine with a rich choice of delicious seafood menus.

Desserts from the region include the famous Tatù (a kind of peppery sweet bread), Panelli di Fiche (fig cakes) and grain based desserts (Ormo di Lupo' cookies and Farringa cake). However, the world's most famous Abruzzi sweets are comfits from Sulmona, which are available in an incredible number of variants and forms.

WHERE TO FIND ABRUZZO SPECIALTIES IN ITALY

BOLOGNA	**L'ORSETTO D'ABRUZZO:** Via Pietralata, 42 - Tel.: 051 295895
FLORENCE	**TRATTORIA DA GIORGIO:** Via Palazzuolo, 100R - Tel.: 055 284302
L'AQUILA	**LA CONCA ALLA VECCHIA POSTA:** Via G. Caldora, 16 - Tel.: 0862 405211
	TRATTORIA LA RUPE: Via San Giacomo, 7 - Tel.: 0862 27481
	OSTERIA ANTICHE MURA: Via XXV Aprile, 2 - Tel.: 0862 62422
MILAN	**IL CAPESTRANO:** Via Gian Francesco Pizzi, 14 - Tel.: 02 5693345
	L'ANGOLO D'ABRUZZO: Via Rosolino Pilo, 20 - Tel.: 02 29406526
	ARCO SEMPIONE: Via Andrea Massena, 1 - Tel.: 02 316102
ROME	**AMBASCIATA D'ABRUZZO:** Via Tacchini, 26 - Tel.: 06 8078256
	L'ABRUZZESE: Via dei Gracchi, 27/29 - Tel.: 06 3973328981
	PICCOLO ABRUZZO: Via Sicilia, 237 - Tel.: 06 42820176
TURIN	**LA CONCA:** Via Assietta, 4 - Tel.: 011 5171091
	TRATTORIA DA CINZIA: Via Madama Cristina, 165 - Tel.: 011 6963515
TRIESTE	**AMBASCIATA D'ABRUZZO:** Via Isidoro Furlani, 6 - Tel.: 040 395050

Frittata di acciughe

Anchovy Frittata

QUICK

EASY

6 whole eggs; 4 anchovy filets deboned and diced together with parsley;
1 clove of crushed garlic; 200g drained tomato chunks;
extra virgin olive oil, salt and hot pepper powder to taste.

Incredibly easy and tasty, this frittata makes a great appetizer - even better with a glass of dry white wine.

PREPARATION

Brown the garlic in a couple tablespoons of oil. As soon as the garlic is golden in colour, remove the clove and pour in the diced anchovy and parsley. Mix in the tomato, hot pepper and a dash of salt. Cook for ten minutes and pour the ingredients in a bowl to cool. After the mixture has cooled, break the eggs into the same bowl; add a little hot pepper and salt and mix. Pour the mixture into a hot well-oiled frying pan and cook without stirring until the bottom turns golden brown. At that point, set an upside-down dinner plate on the frittata and turn the frying pan over so that the frittata rests on the plate. Gently slide the frittata back into the pan and cook the other side. Serve in slices or cubes.

THE LOCAL PRODUCT

TREBBIANO D'ABRUZZO WINE

The production area is very large and includes almost the entire region with hilly areas and high plateaus (no more than 500 meters). The local grape variety has been around quite some time with references that date all the way back to the 16th century. It makes a perfect accompaniment for fresh or saltwater fish as well as legumes, vegetables and eggs.

MODERATE

EASY

Scapece all'uso di Vasto

Vasto-style Scapece

600g of fish fillets; 2 octopus or squid (cleaned); 1 onion sliced very finely; 1 clove of garlic; 1g saffron; mixed herbs (sage, bay, rosemary and others if you like); extra virgin olive oil, flour, strong white wine vinegar, salt and pepper to taste.

An excellent way to preserve seafood and enrich a dinner, this specialty is sold by vendors at markets, fairs and local festivals. It is transported and maintained in wood casks and it is characterized by saffron.

PREPARATION

Cut the molluscs into pieces (including the tentacles). Dry the fish fillets and top the fish and molluscs with salt and pepper, bread in flour and fry in hot oil. When the seafood has turned a golden colour, remove it from the oil and drain on paper towels then place the pieces in a terrine. In the meantime lightly brown the crushed garlic, diced herbs, saffron and a pinch of salt and when it turns golden in colour add a couple of cups of vinegar and simmer until the mixture reduces by around one third. Pour the hot marinade over the seafood (the liquid needs to completely cover the fried pieces) and allow the mixture to marinate in a cool place for at least two days.

THE LOCAL PRODUCT

CONTROGUERRA DOC WINE
The youngest officially recognised Abruzzi D.O.C. wine, Controguerra D.O.C. has a large international market. Cultivated on the hills of Teramo near the border with Le Marche region, the range is complete and extensive.

MODERATE

EASY

Maccheroni alla chitarra

400g maccheroni alla chitarra; 60g pancetta in cubes; 150g ground pork; 1 onion; 500g canned tomatoes; 100g pecorino cheese; hot pepper, oil and salt to taste.

Maccheroni alla chitarra is traditional egg pasta shaped like square spaghetti. In Abruzzo it is generally prepared with mixed meat (beef, pork and lamb) and tomato sauce.

PREPARATION

Cut the pancetta into thin slices and brown it in oil with the diced onion. As soon as the onion begins to turn golden in colour, add the ground meat and hot pepper and brown the mixture a little. Add the canned tomatoes cut into slices, add salt and cook over a very low flame adding a little warm water as needed. Boil the pasta in a large pan of salted water and top with the flavourful meat sauce.

THE LOCAL PRODUCT

PECORINO DI ATRI

Pecorino di Atri is a traditional variety of cheese from an area near the border between the Teramo and Pescara provinces. The cheese has a medium texture, a cylindrical shape and a hazelnut colour. It is moderately sharp.

After aging, the cheese is traditionally preserved under oil. This helps to soften the cheese and gives it a special unique fragrance. Pecorino di Atri makes a perfect appetizer accompanied by bruschetta and olive oil or even as a condiment for pasta.

Minestrone all'uso di Teramo

Teramo-style Minestrone

600g of mixed vegetables (cleaned and sliced); 150g pork rind (well cleaned); 250g of chopped ham or lard (you can also use Ventricina salami), onion, celery and carrot; 200g of ground beef; 100g grated cheese; 250g pasta (small size); 1 egg; extra virgin olive oil, flour, bread crumbs, nutmeg, salt and pepper to taste.

An incredible mix of flavours with the addition of delicious meatballs. These days it even makes a great one-course meal.

PREPARATION

Boil the pork rind for half an hour and in the meantime prepare the meatballs. Mix the meat, egg, bread crumbs (moistened with a little broth or milk) and add salt, pepper and nutmeg. Form the meatballs and roll in flour. Boil the vegetables in salted water and add the chopped mixture and the diced pork rinds when the vegetables are halfway cooked. When the mixture is almost finished, add the pasta and a few minutes later add the meatballs. Serve nice and hot topped with grated cheese.

THE LOCAL PRODUCT

VENTRICINA The Academia Della Ventricina del Vastese in Scerni (C.da Ragna 59, tel. 0873 914173 or 339 3086378), was organised to protect the authenticity of Ventricina against imitations as well as to develop promotional and commercial initiatives.
The traditional processing of pork is still an ongoing tradition amongst farm families throughout the territory. The animal is purchased after being weaned and it is raised on a farm until it reaches a weight of 180-200 kilos. Bran, grain and fruit are the primary forms of feed together with leftovers from the family kitchen. This sort of diet gives the pork a special flavour and ensures its freshness without any additives. The animals are slaughtered during winter since cold weather is fundamental for proper meat processing and more traditional farmers even wait until the moon is waning to begin.

Pesce in brodetto alla pescarese

Pescara-style seafood chowder

MODERATE

EASY

1 ½ Kilos of mixed cleaned seafood (octopus or squid, a few crustaceans, clams and mussels, Monkfish, John Dory, Scorpion Fish); extra virgin olive oil, onion, dried peppers and salt to taste.

This version of the local specialty "brodetto" is a recipe the fisherman use when they are out to sea.

PREPARATION

Thinly slice the onion and cut the dried peppers into strips and brown them both in a lot of olive oil. Allow the mixture to cool and grind with a mortar and pestle. Put the ground mixture back into the pan and add the fish piece by piece (beginning with the pieces that take the most time to cook), salt and cook until it is finished.

THE LOCAL PRODUCT

APRUTINO OIL

The province of Pescara has a wonderful climate for high quality olive oil. The oil is named for the ancient name of this area, which was first known as Aprutium and later as Aprutina. Olives have been cultivated in the area since ancient times with references dating back to the Imperial Era. Moreover, many of the ancient coats of arms of the local families contain an olive tree or branch. In more modern times, the literary works of Gabriele D'Annunzio have provided important testimony of olive cultivation in this area.

TIME CONSUMING

AVERAGE

Tacchino all'uso di Canzano

Canzano-style turkey

This ancient recipe creates a delicate and incredibly aromatic dish. Incredibly easy to store, it was included in the rations during the first lunar expedition!

1 turkey (free-ranging if possible); 4 cloves of garlic; 1 cup of white wine, extra virgin olive oil, rosemary, whole black peppercorns and salt to taste.

PREPARATION

Clean the turkey and divide it in half (remove the breastbone and crush the others). Place the turkey in a deep baking dish and pour boiling salted water over the top, add the herbs and cook in a wood-burning oven for 4 hours. Turn the turkey over and cook for another 4 hours. Serve after at least 12 hours preferably deboned.

THE LOCAL PRODUCT

MONTEPULCIANO D'ABRUZZO WINE

Made from Montepulciano grapes, which were originally from Valle Peligna in Abruzzo, it has no relationship with the Tuscan wine of the same name. It pairs well with robust flavours including pasta with meat sauce, baked or grilled red meats, lamb, pork, game, aged cheeses and flavourful stews. Rosso di Montepulciano is an intense ruby red with touches of violet and a hint of garnet when aged with an aroma of berries and spices.

Ventresca di tonno agli odori

Tuna belly fillets with herbs

4 fresh tuna belly fillets; chopped onion, carrot, celery, garlic and parsley; white wine, extra virgin olive oil, salt to taste.

QUICK

EASY

Easy, aromatic, excellent.

PREPARATION

Heat a few tablespoons of oil in a large shallow pan. Salt and lightly brown the fillets on both sides. Remove the fish from the pan, place on a serving plate and keep warm. Add the chopped herb mixture and lightly brown for 5 minutes then add the wine and simmer. Pour the sauce over the tuna fillet before serving.

THE LOCAL PRODUCT

OIL FROM TERAMO: Olive oil has been cultivated in the province of Teramo since the tenth century BC, but the Romans (third century BC) expanded the cultivation more extensively. Over the course of the centuries, historical events gave rise to periodic ups and downs in production. However, during the Napoleonic census of 1809, photographs were taken to establish the state of olive diffusion in the Teramo province and it has remained almost unchanged today. The quality and popularity of the local olive oil was demonstrated at the International Expo in Vienna in 1873 where it won four first prizes.

TIME CONSUMING

AVERAGE

DESSERT

Ferratelle allo zafferano

Saffron Ferratelle cookies

This is a traditional specialty in Aquila as can be seen by the addition of saffron. To make ferratelle you have to have a special device called a ferratella (hence the name of the cookies), which is similar to a waffle iron and can only be purchased locally.

300g flour; 3 eggs; 2g saffron threads; 60g sugar; extra virgin olive oil and liqueur (orange or anise) to taste.

PREPARATION

Mix the saffron with a little oil. Form the flour into a volcano shape and break the eggs into the hole at the centre. Mix slowly and add the sugar, the saffron oil and a few drops of liqueur. Knead the dough well and then form it into logs that are 3 centimetres in diameter and cut the logs into 3 centimetre sections. Oil and heat the Ferratelle iron and press the dough between the plates, cook for a few seconds and remove it to cool.

THE LOCAL PRODUCT

SAFFRON FROM AQUILA:

Saffron flowers are depicted on Egyptian papyrus scrolls from the second century BC and in the murals of the Minoan palace of Knossos on Crete. Essentially used as a medicinal product originally, it has been used in cooking only since relatively recent times. Saffron was imported to Abruzzo in the thirteen hundreds by Father Santucci. The Dominican monk planted a handful of bulbs he had gathered in Toledo, Spain, in his home town Navelli. They were particularly well-suited for cultivation there and with time saffron from Navelli developed special characteristics that make it different from other varieties. The major source of wealth for over six hundred years alongside sheep farming in the interior Abruzzi lands, it contributed to the economic growth of the city of Aquila in centuries past.

BASILICATA

Basilicata is a small region with large mountains and a small sea coast between Puglia, Campania and Calabria and it is the only path connecting the three. The traditional cuisine fully reflects this geographic reality. There are a number of products and methods of preparation shared by these adjacent lands. In particular there is a strong bond with the Puglia region. Similarly to Puglia, here we find delicious Gnummarieddi or rolls of lamb entrails, Soppressata salami and long-cured prosciutto made from wild or semi-wild black boar. We also see the use of hard grain, freselle hard tack and taralli crackers...

There are numerous specialties. We begin with the Podolica breed of milk cows, which have ancient origins, used to produce Caciocavallo cheese. As far as cheeses are concerned, Canestrato is a highlight: this aged sheep milk cheese is produced outstandingly in the town of Moliterno where they follow a recipe from the 1700s. Another version is made from goat milk. Other worthy products include the sheep cheese from Filiano and the ricotta and buffalo mozzarella, which are excellent but made in small quantities. The pork products are just as fabulous with the prosciutto mentioned above, the famous Lucanica sausage and other local charcuterie specialties.

There is a great deal of attention to bread and hard grain breads in particular: the most famous are from Matera (up to 10 kilos and long-lasting) and Panella from Potenza made from hard grain flour with a golden crispy crust.

However the list of vegetables is just as abundant.

Some of the best include Sarconi beans (white beans similar to the well-known Tuscan zolfino). The list of peppers triumphs with Senise peppers (among the best in Italy) used in a number of different ways including dry for frying and as a paste for topping bread and pasta. Another variety is the Zafran Chin, or Zafarano, a local bell pepper from the San Severino Lucano zone, which can be used in a number of ways (usually powdered) as a condiment. We also find hot spicy peppers used to make an unusual liqueur.

WHERE TO FIND BASILICATA SPECIALTIES IN ITALY

BOLOGNA	**LA FORCHETTA:** Via Caduti della Via Fani, 3 - Tel.: 051 6333999 **RISTORO DEL MERIDIONE:** Via Delle Belle Arti, 6 - Tel.: 051 267648 **SCACCO MATTO:** Via Broccaindosso, 63 - Tel.: 051 263404
GENOA	**L'ANGOLO DELLA LUCANIA:** Via della Libertà, 112 R - Tel.: 010 540063
MILAN	**LA BASILICATA:** Via Emilio De Marchi, 44 - Tel.: 02 37052119 **LA CUCCAGNA:** Via Ponzio, 82 - Tel.: 02 2360296 **TRATTORIA LUCANA DA MARIO:** Via Gluck Cristoforo, 13 - Tel.: 02 6694438
PERUGIA	**LA LOCANDA DEGLI ARTISTI:** Via Campo Battaglia, 10 - Tel.: 075 5735851
POTENZA	**RISTORANTE DA MIMÌ:** Via del Popolo, 115 - Tel.: 0971 1940196 **SOTTAPERA:** Via Delle Belle Arti, 6 - Tel.: 0971 37151 **ZI MINGO:** Via Pierre de Coubertin, 43 - Tel.: 0971 442984
ROME	**LA CANTINA DI NINCO NANCO:** Via Pozzo delle Cornacchie, 36 - Tel.: 06 68135558 **MONTECARUSO:** Via Farini, 12 - Tel.: 06 484436 **OSTERIA GASTONE:** Via Flaminia, 64 - Tel.: 06 36006160

Torta dolce-salata

Sweet and savoury pie

TIME CONSUMING

EASY

200g flour; 120g sugar; 100g butter; 4 eggs; 120g sheep milk ricotta; 60g of a fresh sheep milk caciotta cheese; 1 slice of ham (60g); 1 small mozzarella; 4 tablespoons of grated sheep cheese; extra virgin olive oil and salt to taste.

Fragrant and flavourful, this savoury pie provides a whole new sensation with a touch of sugar blended with other definitively saltier ingredients.

PREPARATION

Mix the flour and sugar, 1 egg, a pinch of salt and the butter cut into pieces. Knead until the dough is blended completely and then cover with a cloth and set aside for 1 hour. In a bowl mix together the ricotta, the caciotta, the mozzarella and the cubed prosciutto, the grated pecorino, 1 whole egg and 1 egg yolk. Roll the dough into two disks and use the larger of the two to line an oiled pan taking care to cover the pan all the way up and over the sides. Pour the mixture into the crust and spread flat with a wooden spoon. Cover the pie with the second smaller crust and fold the edge of the bottom crust over the top. Brush the top of the pie with a well-beaten egg and bake at 180° Celsius for 1 hour.

THE LOCAL PRODUCT

RICOTTA SALATA

In Italian “cotta” means cooked and “ricotta” means “re-cooked”. The cheese is made by re-cooking the whey with additional milk. Ricotta salata is made by dry salting and aging the cheese from 2 months up to a year. The flavour intensifies making it more decisive than classic ricotta. This cheese is great by itself or grated to top pasta or other dishes.

TIME CONSUMING

EASY

Lagane e ciciri

Lagane pasta and chick peas

300g of fresh Lagane pasta (long flat pasta);
600g of chick peas (soaked overnight);
1 clove of garlic; 2 bay leaves; extra virgin olive oil,
hot pepper and salt to taste.

This traditional soup accompanies all the local food events - a local version of the classic Mediterranean pairing of grains and legumes.

PREPARATION

Place the chick peas and the bay leaves in a pan with 2 litres of salted water and cook covered for around 2 hours. The chick peas should be thoroughly cooked but not mushy. In the meantime brown the garlic and a few pieces of hot pepper in olive oil. When the chick peas are finished cooking, boil the pasta in salted water, drain it and pour the pasta, the chick peas and the oil mixture together. Mix and serve.

THE LOCAL PRODUCT

LAGANE
Lagane is a rustic type of pasta that has been around for quite some time. The name derives from the Greek word for pasta "laganon". The ancient dish was most likely quite similar to its modern counterpart. The Romans took the term from Sybaris and Croton, which were colonies of Magna Graecia and latinised it.
In his Satires, Horace nostalgically remembers the food in Venosa his homeland and thinks about lagane and chick peas in particular: the same dish that is popular in neighbourhoods throughout the region today.
This type of pasta is still used throughout the area. One sign of its distinct presence is the curious nickname given to the brigands who terrorised the land and all of southern Italy during the 1800s. They were referred to as "scolalagane" or something like 'lagane drainers'.

Cutturiddi

1.2 Kilos of lamb (deboned and chunked); 400g of cleaned small onions; 1 clove of crushed garlic, rosemary, celery, extra virgin olive oil, salt and pepper to taste.

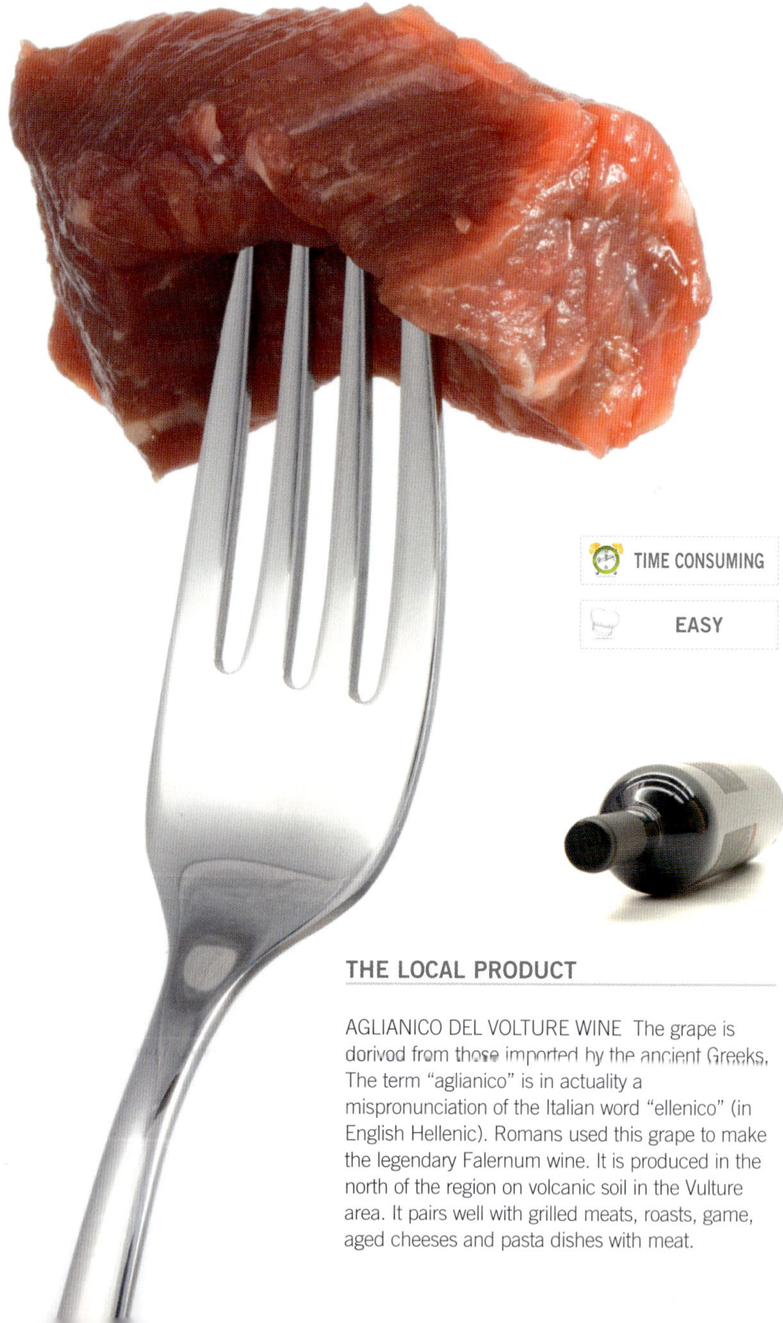

TIME CONSUMING

EASY

Lamb in the spotlight with a flavourful recipe enhanced by a delicious oniony sauce.

PREPARATION

Place all of the ingredients in a large pan and cover with water. Cover the pan and bring to a boil. Lower the flame and simmer for around an hour and a half. It is ready when the liquid has thickened and turned into a creamy sauce.

THE LOCAL PRODUCT

AGLIANICO DEL VOLTURE WINE The grape is derived from those imported by the ancient Greeks. The term "aglianico" is in actuality a mispronunciation of the Italian word "ellenico" (in English Hellenic). Romans used this grape to make the legendary Falernum wine. It is produced in the north of the region on volcanic soil in the Vulture area. It pairs well with grilled meats, roasts, game, aged cheeses and pasta dishes with meat.

Seppioline in umido

Small cuttlefish in sauce

There is not a very long coastline in Basilicata and therefore there is not a plethora of seafood specialties. The dishes are similar to the seafaring specialties served on the adjacent coasts of Calabria and Puglia. This dish, which is common on the Ionian coast, is available along the entire sea coast.

MODERATE

AVERAGE

1 Kilo or more of cleaned cuttlefish;
3 cloves of grated garlic;
500g tomato sauce; 3 anchovy filets
(deboned and chopped); dry white wine,
extra virgin olive oil, chopped parsley,
salt and pepper to taste.

PREPARATION

Cut the cuttlefish into strips, allow them to dry off and brown them in a pan with olive oil, garlic, salt and pepper. After 7-8 minutes, add the wine and the anchovies and simmer. Lower the flame, add the tomato, salt if needed, cover and cook for at least 40 minutes making sure that the sauce does not dry out too much. Top with fresh grated parsley and serve.

THE LOCAL PRODUCT

BREAD FROM MATERA
The main ingredient is remilled durum wheat with a high gluten content. The first stage involves leavening. The flour, salt, sourdough and water are mixed together. The dough rises for around two hours before it is cut and weighed (in 500, 1000 and 2000 gram pieces) and then it is kneaded again by hand and formed into small dough balls that are allowed to rise another 30 minutes. At the end of the second stage, the dough balls are kneaded again to form them into the desired shape (a tall loaf, a tall loaf with slit or a folded loaf "a cornetto"). At that point the loaf is baked and allowed to cool in large baskets. The finished product has a terracotta colour, a straw yellow crumb and it is crispy and fragrant.

Zucchine con peperoni

Zucchini and peppers

MODERATE

EASY

6 zucchini; 4 mint leaves; 30g dried Senise peppers or 100g of fresh peppers; 1 clove of garlic; fresh wild fennel, extra virgin olive oil, salt and pepper to taste.

An incredibly fragrant dish thanks to all the herbs, it is further enhanced by the special taste of Senise peppers.

PREPARATION

Wash the zucchini and cut off the ends. Cut diagonally into oval, very thin slices. Heat one cup of oil in a pan and then lightly brown the garlic (remove the clove when it is golden). Add the sliced zucchini and a piece of wild fennel. Add salt and pepper to taste and cook the zucchini without browning them. Remove the fennel and place the zucchini and liquid in a bowl. Add a large pinch of chopped mint. Complete the dish by adding a handful of dried crushed Senise peppers or fresh finely sliced ones. Serve cool.

THE LOCAL PRODUCT

SENISE BELL PEPPERS

The peppers here are very different from those grown in other areas due to the special soil and environmental conditions which add to their prestige and the quality. The Senise Pepper is planted from the third ten-day period of February to the second ten-day period of March. It is transplanted at the end of May and gathered by hand at the beginning of August when the peppers turn a characteristic red colour. With a thin elongated shape and a low water content, they can be sun-dried easily. The stem does not separate from the pepper after it is dry which makes it possible to tie the dried peppers into characteristic ristras. The peppers are particularly sweet.

'Ncartellate

800g flour; 80g sugar;
80g butter; 4 eggs;
cinnamon or vanilla, honey or
cooked grape must to taste

MODERATE

AVERAGE

Closely related to the more complex "cartellate" from Puglia, 'ncartellate are a tasty sweet treat that make a perfect accompaniment for Christmas time visiting.

PREPARATION

Mix the flour, sugar, butter, egg and a pinch of cinnamon. Knead the dough well. It should be homogenous but not too firm. Roll out a 3 millimetre sheet and cut it into wide strips (around 1½ centimetre). Form the strips into spirals, knots, bows or any form of your choice and deep fry in oil. Drain and place on paper towels. Place them on a serving plate and cover with honey or cooked grape must.

THE LOCAL PRODUCT

MATERA (DOC)
Matera, famous for the ancient homes dug into the rock (known in Italian as the "Sassi") is an extraordinary city offering a plethora of history, art, culture, and folk traditions. The local wine and cuisine offer unique and singular characteristics. The famous durum wheat in Matera has made the local pasta and bread famous. In recent years the Province of Matera, which already produced a large quantity of table grapes, has begun producing wine and this effort led to recognition of the D.O.C. MATERA label. The wine is produced in a number of communities in Matera with Aglianico, Sangiovese, Primitivo, Greco and Malvasia di Basilicata grapes.

CALABRIA

The aim of the local cuisine in Calabria was to preserve the food. Need gave rise to geniality and preserving food was a primary necessity to maintain the freshness of the products in order to make it through the lean times. This gave rise to a number of preparations including charcuterie specialties such as: the famous Capocollo and Soppressata, or the fiery hot 'nduja (or "'ndugghia", from the French word anduille for sausage), a creamy spread of ground pork and pork entrails with wild fennel that is bright red from all the hot pepper - wonderful on bread, as a topping for pasta, or for spicing up soups.

Drying tomatoes was yet another way to preserve food. The tomatoes are baked and sprinkled with herbs and then bottled in olive oil. Fried sardines are preserved under vinegar and oil while the aroma of the Sila forest is captured in bottled mushrooms with varying spice mixtures. Hot peppers are part of all of these processes serving as nature's natural preservative. Hot peppers are so famous in Calabria that they are celebrated at one of the most popular festivals at the beginning of September in Diamante. Here we find hot peppers included in some incredible and yet wonderful combinations (including ice cream, chocolate and beer...) and they are even good for you.

There are no lack of cooling flavours including eggplant and bell peppers (common in many dishes) or the magnificent swordfish or tuna steaks that are popular in Sicily as well. Another famous local specialty is whitebait (locally called neonata, mustica or rosamarina) which are tiny newborn fish preserved under oil with hot pepper. Four very special aromas are highlighted in the local desserts and liqueurs: citron, bergamot orange and liquorice which grow magnificently here and are transformed into high quality products. Staying in theme with sweets, the dried figs are a delightful way to end any dinner.

WHERE TO FIND CALABRIAN SPECIALTIES IN ITALY

BOLOGNA	**OSTERIA DE' COLTELLI DA BIAGIO:** Via De' Coltelli, 6/a - Tel.: 051 223157 **OSTERIA LE MURA:** Vicolo del Falcone, 13 - Tel.: 051 331772 **TRATTORIA VERDE LUNA:** Via Della Guardia, 30 - Tel.: 051 382461
CAGLIARI	**DOLMEN:** Viale Sant'Avendrace, 216 - Tel.: 070 281019
CATANZARO	**PPE' DISPETTU:** Viale Emilia - Località Runc - Tel.: 348 4580487 **TRATTORIA DA SALVATORE:** Prima Salita del Rosario, 28 - Tel.: 0961 724318 **U TAMARRU:** Viale Europa, 28 - Tel.: 0961 751971
FLORENCE	**IL CLARINETTO:** Viale S. Lavagnini, 40 A/B - Tel.: 055 0121050 **PIZZERIA CINZIA:** Via dell'Argin Grosso, 65/N - Tel.: 055 780270
GENOA	**TRATTORIA LE CARAVELLE:** Via Prà 106/R - Tel.: 010 662731
MILAN	**IL PEPERONCINO:** Via Parenzo, 6 - Tel.: 02 89121600 **OSTERIA CALABRESE:** Via della Chiesa Rossa, 111 - Tel.: 02 84895050 **RISTORANTE DONGIÒ:** Via Bernardino Corio, 3 - Tel.: 02 5511372
PALERMO	**IL PICCOLO DIAVOLO:** Via Danimarca, 21/23 - Tel.: 091 2523098
ROME	**LA N'DUJA:** Piazza S. M. Consolatrice, 1/4 - Tel.: 06 4370025 **LA PECORA PAZZA:** Via Statilia, 35 - Tel.: 06 7011637 **RISTORANTE LE MASCHERE:** Via del Monte della Farina, 29 - Tel.: 06 68309531
TURIN	**IN VINO VERITAS:** Via Giulia di Barolo, 50 - Tel.: 347 0109214 **QUATTRO SOLDI:** Corso Castelfidardo, 7 - Tel.: 011 5621290

Licurdia

QUICK

EASY

1 litre vegetable broth; 1 cube of lard; 4 red Tropea onions; 50g of grated sheep-milk cheese from Crotone; dry crusty bread; hot spicy pepper and salt to taste.

THE LOCAL PRODUCT

TROPEA ONIONS

Onions were already being cultivated in northern Asia and Palestine 5000 years ago. During the Peloponnesian War onions were used as rations for the soldiers. By grating the onions and mixing them with honey, they even created a fermented beverage like mead. Its culinary uses during Medieval and Renaissance times are well documented in recipe books of the day. The red onion was imported to Calabria by the Phoenicians a mere 2000 years ago. At the beginning of the eighteen hundreds one of the most interesting and oldest documents on the economy of southern Italy (written by Gioacchino Murat) stated that red Tropea onions were a precious resource for the region.

This intensely flavoured soup is homage to the magnificent red Tropea onions.

PREPARATION

Peel the onions and place them in cold water for half an hour. Finely slice the onions and brown them in a ceramic pan with the lard. Add the vegetable broth and continue cooking for at least a half hour over a medium flame. Before serving, grill a few pieces of dry bread that have been rubbed with hot pepper. Use the grilled bread to line ceramic serving dishes and pour the onion mixture over it and top with a handful of grated sheep-milk cheese.

TIME CONSUMING

AVERAGE

FIRST COURSES

Millecosedde

400g Savoy cabbage; 300g of cleaned mushrooms; 50 g of pancetta; 200g of each of the following types of dry legumes: fava beans, beans, lentils, chick peas; 80g of grated cheese; 200g small soup pasta; extra virgin olive oil and salt to taste.

Magnificent minestrone with the best winter has to offer to help pick up your spirits and ward of the cold.

PREPARATION

Soak the legumes (separately) for as long as required. Cut the cabbage into strips and boil in a little salted water. Boil the legumes in salted water as long as required (the bigger beans take more time and should be added first) and then brown the pancetta chunks in a large deep pan with oil. When the pancetta is golden brown, add the legumes, the drained cabbage and the sliced mushrooms. Fill the pan with water and add salt and pepper and boil. When the mixture boils, add the pasta to the broth, check the salt and pepper and cook the pasta. Serve in bowls topped with extra virgin olive oil and grated cheese.

THE LOCAL PRODUCT

OLIVE OIL FROM CROTONE

In the province of Crotone the cultivation of olives for oil dates back to around 2000 years before Christ. However, the first documented references date back the byzantine era and a group of Basilian monks who escaped to Calabria towards the end of the sixth century and worked to improve local olive cultivation techniques. The discoveries of ancient oil mills (sixth to tenth century AD) are evidence of their work as are the centuries-old olive trees near where they settled. At the start of the eighteen hundreds a Cerenzian nobleman named Francesco Benincasa wrote to the inspector of Cosenza and the Società Agraria of the Kingdom of the Two Sicilies about the local flora saying that the olive trees were worthy of attention because they grew well and produced amazing products. As long as anyone can remember the harvest season has begun with the festival of Cullurello where they serve Cullurello fritters fried in the newly harvested oil, which are eaten alongside dressed olives.

TIME CONSUMING

DIFFICULT

Sagne chine

400g flour; 200g ground beef; 4 eggs; 150g of each of the following: sliced onions, steamed green peas, cleaned artichokes sliced and steamed, mushrooms sliced and steamed; 150g of soft cheese; 2 bay leaves; 80g of grated sheep-milk cheese; lard, extra virgin olive oil, salt and pepper to taste.

This casserole is a festival in itself: absolutely full of fragrant flavour (in local dialect sagne chine means full lasagne).

PREPARATION

Make a rather firm dough from flour, a little warm water and a pinch of salt and then put the dough in a bowl, cover it and set it aside. After around 1 hour, roll out a sheet of dough and cut square pieces measuring 8 centimetres on each side and boil them in salted water. Drain the pasta when it is al dente and set it on a smooth kitchen towel to dry. In the meantime mix the ground beef with the egg yolk, salt and pepper. Make tiny meatballs with the mixture, roll them in flour and deep fry the meatballs in oil aromatized with bay, then drain them and set aside. Add the lard and brown the onion, peas, artichokes and mushrooms. Grease a baking pan with lard and alternate layers of pasta, layers with pieces of hard-boiled egg and soft cheese, layers with meat balls and vegetables, topping each layer with grated cheese. Cook in the oven at 220 Celsius until it forms a lovely crust.

THE LOCAL PRODUCT

PECORINO FROM CROTONE

A well known classic, the pecorino is produced exclusively with milk from Gentile breed sheep and goat rennet. It is aged from 4 months to two years in a cool place at a constant temperature. During the aging process, the forms are oiled with olive oil. It is one of the most popular cheeses in Calabria and it is produced in the province of Crotone. In time, the cheese becomes drier and the flavour grows sharper. The pecorino cheese is great plain, as an appetizer or together with sun-dried tomatoes, local salami and vegetables in oil which are popular local specialties. It is also great grated and sprinkled on top first courses with spicy meat sauces.

Schiaffettoni

400g flour; 4 eggs; 200g ground beef;
150g of mixed diced salami and sausage;
2 hard-boiled eggs (mashed with a fork);
300g of simple pasta sauce; 4 tablespoons of chopped onion, carrot and celery; 80g of grated sheep-milk cheese; extra virgin olive oil, salt and pepper to taste.

TIME CONSUMING

MODERATE

A great first course for holidays stuffed pasta with a rich filling that is admirably balanced by the simplicity of the sauce.

PREPARATION

Mix the flour, eggs, one tablespoon of oil and a pinch of salt. Form dough, knead it well and set aside in a dish covered with a cloth. In the meantime, brown the diced herbs and add the beef and diced meats and brown. Finally add the hard-boiled eggs and a dash of salt and pepper. Roll out a thin sheet of dough and cut into rectangular pieces (about 8x10 cm.). At the centre of each piece of pasta place a spoonful of the filling and then close it on the short side and seal the borders well. Boil the shiaffettoni pasta in salted water and drain after 7-8 minutes. Serve in layers topping each layer with some of the sauce and sheep-milk cheese ending with sauce and cheese on the top.

THE LOCAL PRODUCT

SALAMI FROM CALABRIA:
The origin of salami from Calabria dates back to the Greek colonisation of the Ionian Coast and the cultural opulence of Magna Graecia while historical references that describe pork processing date to the beginning of the 17th century. The first reference was in a work entitled "Della Calabria Illustrata" (Calabria Illustrated) that mentioned the widespread use of special processing techniques for pork. In more recent times, the production of cured meats in Calabria was documented in the census statistics during the era of Gioacchino Murat (the beginning of the nineteenth century). Those documents describe the use of spices and aromas derived from local plants to give the meat more flavour. One of the most famous testimonials of Calabrian cured meats was Giacomo Casanova. In his memoirs he remembers having had lunch during his tour of Calabria at the cafeteria of Bishop Francescantonio Cavalcanti where he tasted Calabrian charcuterie specialties and judged them to be the best he had ever eaten.

DESSERT

Nepitelle

For the dough: 500g flour; 1 sachet of yeast; 150g butter (or lard); 150g sugar; 3 eggs

For the filling: the zest of 2 oranges; 30g of unsweetened cocoa powder; 2 teaspoons of cinnamon; ½ teaspoon of powdered cloves; 100g of dark chocolate; 150g of dried figs; 200g almonds; 200g honey; 200g walnuts; 1 shot of Strega liqueur; 150g of raisins; 200g of Vino Cotto (or cherry jam)

MODERATE | **AVERAGE**

Nepitelle cookies are a traditional Easter specialty. The name derives from the Latin term nepitedum which means eyelids. The shape of this dessert is reminiscent of a closed eyelid.

PREPARATION

Prepare the dough first. Form the flour and sugar into a volcano shape and break the eggs into the hole at centre, then add the softened butter and the yeast. Knead very well until the dough is even and smooth. Roll out the dough with a rolling pin until it reaches a thickness of 2mm and with a pasta cutter or a pizza cutter, cut out disks of dough about the size of your palm. Prepare the filling by softening the raisins in warm water and chopping the nuts, almonds, figs and dark chocolate. Pour the chopped ingredients into a large bowl, drain the raisins and add the cocoa powder, spices, grated orange zest, a shot of rum or Strega liqueur, the vino cotto (or cherry jam) and honey to make a soft but firm mixture. Brush the borders of the dough disks with egg white (to help them seal) and then put a bit of the filling in the centre of each one and fold it in half to form a half circle and press with a fork to close the edges. Brush the nepitelle with egg yolk and set on a baking pan lined with oven paper and bake at 200° Celsius for around 30 minutes or until golden.

THE LOCAL PRODUCT

CLEMENTINES FROM CALABRIA

Clementines from Calabria have no seeds; they are an intensely orange colour and have a succulent, sweet aromatic pulp. They are easy to peel and have a perfect balance between sweet and sour. Clementines are refreshing, diuretic and they contain a high level of available sugars. They can be eaten plain or used to prepare fruit juice, syrup, sorbet and jam. The fruit is also used in cosmetics as an ingredient in tonic creams and masques for the skin. The cultivation of Clementines began after 1950 in Calabria – and it makes a perfect natural habitat.

TIME CONSUMING

DIFFICULT

Pitta della Madonna

500g flour; 2 eggs; 150g raisins (soaked in warm water); 200g chopped walnuts; 200g sugar; 1 lemon; 1 orange; 8 tablespoons of lard; ½ cup of Vino Cotto (or cherry jam); cinnamon powder, extra virgin olive oil and salt to taste.

This specialty is served on May 8th to celebrate the Feast of the Virgin Mary. The local version in Crotone is a true expression of love considering the time and care this dessert requires to be transformed into a bouquet of May roses in honour of the Virgin Mary.

THE LOCAL PRODUCT

LA PITTA 'MPIGLIATA
In times past when being able to celebrate an event was a luxury reserved to very few, the farmers in the Sila area invented their own dessert using the products that were available and on hand. They took almonds, walnuts and raisins and decided to encase them in a pastry sheet. As the years passed and the farmers' palates became more refined that ancient rustic and exquisite dessert was enhanced with natural aromas (cloves, cinnamon, dried orange zest, fortified wine) giving rise to Pitta 'Mpigliata.

PREPARATION

Mix the flour and eggs, 50g sugar, a pinch of salt and grated lemon zest. Mix until there are no lumps and divide the mixture into two unequal parts measuring one third and two thirds of the total mixture. Use the larger part to create two sheets of dough (not too thin) around 60 centimetres in diameter. Spread a little oil (or cooked grape must) on the dough sheet and sprinkle with walnuts and raisins topped with cinnamon, orange zest and sugar. Cover with the other sheet of dough and press down on the edges delicately with your hands to seal it. Cut strips of dough (2-3 centimetres wide) and form a rosette with each one by rolling it (taking care that the filling does not fall out). With the remaining dough roll out another sheet and place it on a well oiled baking pan. Place the rosettes on the dough so that they touch one another and pull up the edges of the bottom dough sheet to form a basket around the rosettes. Cover with sugar and bake at 200° C for around ½ an hour.

CAMPANIA

Local cuisine in the Campania region is a triumph of creativity and not only for the peoples' proverbial skill at getting by, which is a common trait in poor food, it is also due to the thoroughly Neapolitan penchant for joy, colour and brilliance. The result is an incredibly varied cuisine that is rich in fillings and pairings that enhance the local flavours to the maximum. Even flavours that arrived from afar have triumphed here. One case is the tomato, which was imported from America in the 1500s. However it was so well used by Neapolitan cooks that it has become the symbol of local cuisine. And what would pizza or pasta be without magnificent tomato sauce on top or 'pummarola 'n coppa' as they say in local dialect. Pasta shares a similar story. It was invented elsewhere – most likely China – but on the slopes of Mount Vesuvius it took root and has reaped success the world over.

It is true that Neapolitan cooks have had many opportunities to get to know different cooking styles and recipes. Having been under the control of both Spain and France sparked the local culinary imagination. We find traces of that in Scapece, which derives from the Spanish Escabeche and the French-sounding Sartù (an amazing rice casserole with a rich filling) or the babà (fluffy cakes soaked in rum). However, these dishes were transformed so well in the wise hands of Neapolitan cooks that for years people have been singing their praises and nobody remembers the progenitors any longer.

Part of the merit for the incredible abundance goes to the richness of the tasty ingredients which are the result of a favourable climate and good soil. The fine selection of local vegetables includes the magnificent San Marzano tomato and lemons from the Amalfi coast. The range of fine cheeses is topped by provolone, burrini and provolette stuffed with peppers and olives as well as fresh cheeses (the buffalo mozzarella is truly a delight). The list goes on with historic traditional pasta dishes, an incredible reserve of fresh fish from the Tyrrhenian Sea and dried fruits. With specialties like babà, struffoli, sfogliatelle and pastiera the only problem with dessert is having to choose.

WHERE TO FIND CAMPANIA SPECIALTIES IN ITALY

ANCONA	**RISTORANTE TRAIANO:** Via XXIX Settembre, 6/A - Tel.: 071 2073634
AOSTA	**PIZZERIA BELLA NAPOLI:** Via Silvano Lucat, 6 - Tel.: 0165 40651
BARI	**NAPUL'È:** Via Crisanzio, 47 - Tel.: 080 2071044
BOLOGNA	**LA PARANZA:** Piazza VII Novembre 1944, 2/A - Tel.: 051 522002
CAGLIARI	**SCIUÈ SCIUÈ:** Via de S'Ecca Manna - Tel.: 070 2347102
CAMPOBASSO	**LA LOCANDA DI PULCINELLA:** Via Marconi Guglielmo, 132 - Tel.: 0874 842177
FLORENCE	**PIZZERIA FUNICULÌ:** Via il Prato, 83/R - Tel.: 055 2646553
GENOA	**LA PIEDIGROTTA:** Via A. Gianelli, 29 - Tel.: 010 3200561
MILAN	**FRIJENNO E MAGNANNO:** Via Benedetto Marcello, 93 - Tel.: 02 29403654 **IL DOGE DI AMALFI:** Via Sangallo, 41 - Tel.: 02 730286
NAPLES	**ANTICA PIZZERIA PORT'ALBA:** Via Port'Alba, 18 - Tel.: 081 459713 **L'EUROSOLDINO:** Via Carlo de Cesare, 59 - Tel.: 081 413925 **RISTORANTE LE ANCORE:** Calata Villa del Popolo - Tel.: 081 5535235
PALERMO	**NEAPOLIS:** Via Belgio, 41 - Tel.: 091 524477
PERUGIA	**QUATTRO PASSI:** Via Bartolo, 25 - Tel.: 075 5716120
PESCARA	**NAPUL'È:** Viale G. Marconi, 14 - Tel.: 085 4510599
POTENZA	**U' SARACINO:** Via Costa Gaveta - Tel.: 0971 1800476
ROME	**AL VECCHIO LOTTO:** Via Veio, 43/45 - Tel.: 06 7003643 **L'AMBASCIATA DI CAPRI:** Via Ennio Quirino Visconti, 52 - Tel.: 06 89928793
TURIN	**DON GENNARO:** Piazza Crispi, 52 - Tel.: 011 2876296
TRIESTE	**MASCALZONE LATINO:** Via Cavana, 12 - Tel.: 040 313332
VENICE	**AL CARDINALE:** Via Miranese, 358 - Tel.: 041 5246897

Mozzarella in carrozza

16 slices of dry bread sliced thin; 1 buffalo mozzarella (around 300g); 3 eggs; bread crumbs; extra virgin olive oil, milk, salt and pepper to taste.

Like many Neapolitan recipes, mozzarella in carrozza is very popular in many places. The risk is that we get used to eating somewhat quick approximate versions (this has already happened with pizza). It is worth the trouble to go for authenticity.

PREPARATION

Cut the crust off of the bread slices and sprinkle them with a little milk, salt and pepper. Place a slice of mozzarella on half of the bread slices and then cover them with the others to make a sandwich. Take care that the pieces stay in place as you dip them in an egg beaten with salt and then in bread crumbs. Deep fry until it is golden brown on both sides. Drain on paper towels and serve immediately.

QUICK

EASY

THE LOCAL PRODUCT

LA MOZZARELLA

Originally due to being perishable, mozzarella was produced in small quantities and eaten locally. It was considered as a by-product of provola cheese and it did not receive much attention due to the fact that it was hard to preserve and sell since it is eaten fresh and therefore it was destined to a very few possibly refined palates. The etymology of the word mozzarella comes from the Italian word 'mozza' meaning to dock or cut off (this is the final process in making mozzarella). In the most ancient references mozzarella is frequently referred to directly as 'mozza' or provatura. In the second half of the 1700s mozzarella became more common at markets in Naples. It spread with the diffusion of the roadways and after the unification of Italy a famous "Taverna" was created between Naples and Caserta in Aversa to serve as a wholesale market for buffalo mozzarella and ricotta. The prices were established daily based on the production and demand quotas.

MODERATE

EASY

Pizza Margherita

500g flour; 1 cube of brewer's yeast; 250g mozzarella (buffalo if possible); 200g tomato chunks; extra virgin olive oil, oregano, basil and salt to taste

The origin of this pizza lies somewhere between history and legend. It is said that a Neapolitan cook made this pizza for Queen Margherita of Savoy as a colourful tribute (red, white and green are the colours of Italy and of the pizza). This classic pizza is very simple and loved the world over. The few essential ingredients make it light and suited to all palates.

THE LOCAL PRODUCT

"COLATE" ANCHOVY SAUCE

Cetara is a fishing town with excellent local anchovies that have always served as an important local resource. Eaten fresh when they are in season, they are preserved under oil when fishing is not possible - so why not try to use that fragrant sauce at the bottom of the bottle when the anchovies are finished? And the people did find a way to perfect the conservation process: layers of anchovies are covered with salt and layered with herbs (garlic, oregano, hot pepper and wild fennel are musts) then covered in extra virgin olive oil and closed in canning jars for around a month to season in the September sun. At that point the jar is opened, the ingredients are mixed and the solids run through a press. It is set aside again and at the beginning of winter the actual sauce is made by filtering the ingredients. One spoonful of the tasty sauce makes a perfect condiment for fragrant spaghetti or a great addition to Neapolitan pizza.

PREPARATION

Mix the brewer's yeast in a glass of warm water. Pour the flour onto a dough board and form a volcano shape with a hole at the centre and pour the water and yeast into it together with salt and a tablespoon of oil. Knead well until the dough is smooth. Form a dough ball and set it aside in a warm dry place until it has doubled in volume. In the meantime cut the mozzarella into chunks and squeeze it to remove any excess liquid. Roll out a round crust that fits the size of your pizza pan. Oil the pan and sprinkle it with a little flour before laying the crust on top and stretching it out gently with your fingertips. Then top the pizza with the tomato sauce, mozzarella, oregano, basil, salt and a dash of oil. Bake in a preheated oven at 220° Celsius for about twenty minutes.

FIRST COURSES

Sartù di riso

Rice Sartù

250g of rice for risotto; ½ litre of tomato sauce; 1 sausage; 100g grated parmesan; 2 eggs (one of them hard-boiled); 10g of dried funghi porcini mushrooms soaked in warm water; 300g of pancetta; 200g of green peas; 1 onion; 150g of ground beef; 2 slices of dry white bread softened in milk; 200g of mozzarella; ½ litre of broth (meat or bouillon); bread crumbs, butter, extra virgin olive oil, salt and pepper to taste.

TIME CONSUMING | DIFFICULT

This incredibly elaborate dish is one of the magnificent baked first course specialties destined to important occasions. It is a part of Neapolitan cuisine that developed during the 1700s in the courts of the French nobility but the local distinction is unmistakable in the aroma and fragrance. It makes a perfectly complete one-course meal.

PREPARATION

Brown a diced onion and the sausage in a pan. Add the tomato, salt and cover the pan and simmer on a low flame for at least 1 hour. After cooking, cut the sausage into pieces. In the meantime peel the hard-boiled egg and cut it into thin slices. Then prepare the meatballs by mixing the ground beef with the softened bread, 1 egg, 2 tablespoons of parmesan, salt and pepper. Make tiny meatballs and fry them in oil. In another pan brown a few slices of onion and the diced pancetta, then add the peas and sliced mushrooms and cook for around ten minutes. Now you need to prepare the risotto. Gently brown a few slices of onion and add the dry rice and continue cooking until the rice begins to turn transparent. Add the broth and half of the sauce and keep cooking and adding broth or warm water. When the rice is finished cooking, remove it from the stove and mix in grated parmesan and stir well. Butter a Bundt cake pan and cover the bottom and sides with breadcrumbs. Place a layer of risotto, a layer of meatballs and mozzarella and top it with tomato and meat sauce (do not use all of the sauce). Now add the peas and mushrooms, the sausage and egg and cover with grated parmesan. Place the remaining rice on top and press it down and cover with more grated parmesan. Top with breadcrumbs and a few pats of butter. Bake at 180° Celsius for around 20 minutes. After cooking, remove the rice from the pan, cut into slices and serve with a few spoonfuls of the remaining sauce.

THE LOCAL PRODUCT

CILENTO OLIVE OIL

The lands around Cilento are covered in olives which are the primary, and sometimes only local resource making it an integral part of everyday community life. Olives have been cultivated in Cilento since the times of the ancient Magna Graecia colonies and continued after the lands were overtaken by the Roman Empire. It was the people of Phocaea (of Greek origins) that introduced the most ancient variety of oil. Known as Pisciottana, it is resistant to insects and is hardy in the salty local winds and very productive even on arid land. It is still used and gives Cilento oil its characteristic qualities.

QUICK

EASY

Timballo di maccheroni

Macaroni Casserole

350g macaroni; 300 ml of meat and tomato sauce; 20g grated parmesan; 200ml béchamel sauce; 300g mozzarella; basil; butter; bread crumbs to taste.

Born as a way to use leftover pasta this casserole is a tasty and creative dish.

PREPARATION

Cook the macaroni in a large pot of salted water and drain the pasta when it is still very al dente. Mix the pasta with the tomato and meat sauce, the béchamel and grated parmesan. Cut the mozzarella in chunks and add half of it to the macaroni. Butter a baking ban and then cover in bread crumbs. Preheat the oven to 180° Celsius. Pour the macaroni in the casserole dish and add a little more sauce and the rest of the mozzarella. Add a little basil and bake in the oven (lower the temperature to 160°) for around 15-20 minutes. Open the oven door, but leave the pan in the oven to keep the pasta warm while the sauce thickens.

THE LOCAL PRODUCT

AGLIANICO DEL TABURNO WINE
The wine is produced on the sunny Sannio hills including 13 municipalities between the slopes of Monte Taburno and the valley of the Calore River. The local wine producers began with aglianico, which has rich and ancient origins to further extend the range with primarily native grapes.

TIME CONSUMING

AVERAGE

Braciolone napoletano

1 large beefsteak (600g); 3 eggs;
50g of prosciutto crudo (dry-cured ham);
1 kilo of ripe sauce tomatoes; 50g of raisins and pine nuts; 1 cup of white wine; 1 onion;
2 garlic cloves; parsley, oregano, nutmeg, basil, extra virgin olive oil, salt and pepper to taste.

Alongside the "poor" recipes made from scraps or leftovers, which formed the major part of poorer families' diets, we also find sumptuous, excessive recipes filled with rich ingredients. These were daily specialties for the upper ranks of society and for everybody on special occasions and holidays. The following recipe is definitely part of the second group of recipes.

PREPARATION

Hard boil the eggs and cut into slices. Cover the steak with salt, pepper and nutmeg then cover it with the ham, the egg slices and diced garlic, parsley and oregano, raisins and pine nuts. Roll up the steak and tie it tightly with kitchen string. Gently brown thin onion slices in oil and then add the meat and brown on all sides before adding the wine. Add the wine and cook until it evaporates then and add the tomato, basil, salt and pepper. Lower the flame, cover the pan and cook for at least 1½ hours. The sauce is also wonderful for topping pasta.

THE LOCAL PRODUCT

SAN MARZANO TOMATOES

The ideal local conditions are one of the reasons San Marzano tomatoes are so good. The soil is volcanic and the climate is positively influenced by the sea. The plant is grown vertically so that the fruits do not touch the ground and remain perfectly unmarred. The tomatoes are gathered exclusively by hand when they are completely mature. San Marzano tomatoes have an elongated prism shape around 60 to 80mm long. They are juicy and almost seedless and the skin is smooth and easy to remove. The flavour and the aroma are unmistakeable. The mature tomato can be kept in the refrigerator for almost ten days at a temperature of 1-2° Celsius. If the tomatoes are canned, they should be kept in a closed glass container in the refrigerator after having been opened. They are wonderful with seafood dishes and all sorts of simple traditional dishes that form the basis of the Mediterranean diet.

TIME CONSUMING

AVERAGE

DESSERT

Babà

240g flour;
180g butter; 4 eggs;
1 cup of milk;
200g of simple syrup;
140g sugar; 1 small glass of rum;
20g of brewer's yeast

They are traditionally believed to have been invented at the magnificent Polish court and were personally attributed to King Stanislaw Leszczynski who in turn attributes them to a pre-existing Polish dessert that he simply dipped in rum. Around Naples, the babà is much more than a simple dessert, it has become a ritual and philosophy of life. It is a common expression to define the best of something in a certain field. Though seemingly simple, this dessert is tasty and refined.

PREPARATION

Dissolve the yeast in a cup of warm water. Mix it with the flour and make a dough ball. Allow the dough to raise in a warm oven until it has doubled. Then add the eggs, butter and remaining milk and pour the mixture into buttered babà baking pans. Let them raise again and then bake at 200° for 20 minutes. As soon as they have cooled top them well with simple syrup mixed with rum.

THE LOCAL PRODUCT

GRECO DI TUFO
This grape, which originated in Thessaly, reached the Campania countryside somewhere around the sixth century BC following Greek colonisation. There is a reference from 100 BC in a fresco at Pompeii where a "Greek wine" is explicitly mentioned. The grapes are cultivated on the slopes of Mt. Vesuvius and later spread throughout the province of Avellino where it took the name "di Tufo" from a city at the centre of the production area. The white is perfect with crustaceans, funghi porcini mushroom risotto, delicate fish and fresh cheeses. The bubbly spumante version is great as an aperitif or with cold appetizers.

TIME CONSUMING

DIFFICULT

Pastiera

For the crust: 250g butter; 2 eggs; 50g honey; 150g powdered sugar; 4g salt; 5g baking powder; 500g flour
For the filling: 600g ricotta; 600g sugar; 1 vanilla bean; 1 spoonful of orange flower extract; 550g of cooked grain; 1 teaspoon of cinnamon; 3 eggs; 1 orange; 1 lemon; ½ cup of Strega liqueur, 200g of custard; 40g of candied orange.

This is a famous Easter dessert in Naples and locally it is an essential part of the return of spring to be shared by all the families. In past times they began cooking the grain for the dessert on the Thursday before Easter. These days in Naples and elsewhere, most people use grain prepared by specialised pastry shops, however bottles of it are also available in stores.

PREPARATION

For the crust, mix and knead the ingredients for 3 minutes. Form a dough ball, wrap it in plastic wrap and place in the refrigerator overnight. In a bowl, mix the ricotta with sugar, vanilla, a few drops of orange flower extract and mix vigorously. Add the cooked grain, the cinnamon, two egg yolks, grated orange and lemon zest, two eggs whites beaten until stiff and a drop of liqueur. Mix well as you add the custard and the candied oranges. Butter a pan and cover it with the rolled-out dough and pour the filling on top. Use the extra dough to decorate the top and brush it lightly with egg yolk. Bake in the oven for 40 minutes. Cover with powdered sugar before serving.

THE LOCAL PRODUCT

AMALFI LEMONS Lemons have been present in Naples since very ancient times as can be seen by the paintings and mosaics of them at the excavations in Pompeii and Herculaneum. Cultivation of lemons on the Amalfi coast grew more than all the other areas. Lemons have been growing on these splendid cliffs over the sea since the 11th century when the Amalfi Republic published a decree requiring all ships to have lemons aboard due to having discovered its effectiveness in combating illnesses caused by low vitamin C. That drove the planting of lemon groves between the 12th and 14th century on more areas near the sea and nearby hills. The first large lemon market dates back to the sixteen hundreds. That grew over the centuries and sold to traders from other areas that purchased nearly all of their merchandise.

MODERATE

AVERAGE

300g flour; 2 whole eggs and 1 yolk; 40g butter; 1 tablespoon sugar; 200g honey; ½ cup liqueur (limoncello, rum or brandy); 30g of each of the following: candied orange, candied citron and candied squash; grated lemon zest, salt, extra virgin olive oil, coloured comfits and/or cinnamon comfits to taste.

DESSERT

Struffoli

In Naples it is not Christmas without the smell of struffoli in the air and colouring the tables with classic comfits called "diavulilli". We propose the classic recipe, but these days many people use leavened dough because they prefer fluffier softer struffoli. In this case, just add a little baking soda and let it rise.

PREPARATION

Combine the flour, egg, butter, sugar, lemon zest, liqueur and a pinch of salt in a bowl and mix well. After mixing set aside for ½ hour. After that, knead the dough again briefly and divide it into balls the size of an apple. Roll the dough on a floured surface to create dough logs that are around 1 centimetre thick. Cut the logs into little bits of dough. Heat the oil and deep-fry the struffoli (not too many all at once). Remove them from the oil when they are fluffy and golden. Remove them with a slotted spoon and place on paper towels. In the meantime heat the honey in a double boiler until it becomes very liquid and then add the struffoli stir delicately until they are all covered in honey. Add most of the candied fruit and comfits and mix. Top with the rest of the candied fruits and comfits.

THE LOCAL PRODUCT

FIANO DI AVELLINO WINE
This wine also has an ancient history. It was mentioned in the records of Frederick II of Svevia and in the vineyards planted by Carlo d'Angio. The production area includes 26 municipalities in Irpinia including the capital Avellino. It has a cool sunny climate and a well-structured soil that is perfect for the grape. Wonderful as an aperitif or to accompany traditional desserts, the wine is also magnificent with crustaceans, squid and fish dishes as well as fresh cheeses.

EMILIA ROMAGNA

Tagliatelle, tortelli, ravioli, cappelletti, tagliolini, lasagne, agnolini, cappellacci, garganelli, cannelloni... endless forms and infinite flavours render homage to the majesty of egg pasta - unbeatable here both in quality and variety. It has a firm and elastic consistency due to the many eggs and the masterful skill of generations of cooks. Emilia is more countryside and Romagna is more seaside but egg pasta triumphs throughout the region, though where it is best and where it originated may be debated. By following the preparations we can trace an outline of the culinary map of the territory. The traditional topping for many egg pasta dishes is meat sauce (Bolognese sauce) and parmesan cheese is a must – whether sprinkled on top or mixed in the filling: this local cheese is famous throughout the world. In the fillings we find various cuts of pork and the jealously guarded recipes vary from one town to the next. There is no shortage of vegetable fillings including squash or spinach. Egg pasta is used to make inspired first courses that render homage to the Adriatic Sea. Pasta is even used to make a dessert, torta di taglierini (thin tagliatelle cake). And if more is better just consider cannelloni filled with tortellini: a true declaration of love for egg pasta.

Having said all this, we have not even begun to scratch the surface of the cuisine in Emilia Romagna. Regional tables are filled with specialties that are so good they have become known and loved beyond regional borders. Just consider the famous piadina flat bread (or crescentina - a fried variety that makes a tasty snack) or the refined balsamic vinegar and the countless types of salami where the local creativity truly went wild: prosciutto, culatello, mortadella, coppa, zampone, cotechino, salama da sugo, spalla, salami and lard... and each one has scores of variations. However, instead of listing the many delicious specialties, it makes more sense to highlight the spirit that gave rise to them: the desire to calmly, creatively, skilfully and enjoyably explore the pleasure of this land.

WHERE TO FIND EMILIA ROMAGNA SPECIALTIES IN ITALY

BOLOGNA	**IL MULINO BRUCIATO:** Via della Selva Pescarola, 50 - Tel.: 051 6343072 **OSTERIA BOCCA BUONA:** Via degli Usberti, 5 - Tel.: 051 221750 **TRATTORIA CASA BUIA:** Via dell'Arcoveggio, 138 - Tel.: 051 320089
GENOA	**CUCINA EMILIANA:** Via Soliman 35/R - Tel.: 010 6501885
MILAN	**DA MAURO IL BOLOGNESE:** Via Elia Lombardini, 14 - Tel.: 02 8372866 **GNOCCO FRITTO:** Via Pasquale Paoli, 2 - Tel.: 02 58100216 **OSTERIA BORSIERI:** Via Pietro Borsieri, 39 - Tel.: 02 6070800
ROME	**LA LOCANDA:** Via Massaciuccoli, 26 - Tel.: 06 86207499 **LE COLLINE EMILIANE:** Via degli Avignonesi, 22 - Tel.: 06 4817538 **RISTORANTE EMILIA ROMAGNA:** Via Ostiense, 36/H - Tel.: 06 81109052
TURIN	**OSTERIA PARMA VECCHIA:** Via Beinasco, 5 - Tel.: 011 859323

Scarpazoun

MODERATE

AVERAGE

200g flour; 1 kilo of cleaned spinach or swiss chard; 100g of grated parmesan; 100g of diced lard; 100g of pancetta unrolled and cut into cubes; 1 small chopped onion; 1 clove of crushed garlic; butter, extra virgin olive oil, salt and pepper to taste.

A savoury pie – also known as erbazzone – that is a local specialty in Reggio Emilia and was a favourite for picnics. These days it is also used as an appetizer or snack.

PREPARATION

Boil and drain the vegetables (squeeze out as much water as possible) and then chop. Gently brown the garlic, onion and lard and then add the vegetables. Stir and cook for around 5 minutes. When the mixture has cooled, add the parmesan, a little oil and a pinch of pepper. In a separate container mix the flour, salt and water and knead into dough. Roll out two sheets of dough (one a few centimetres larger in diameter). Oil the pan and lay the larger crust on the pan folding the borders up at the edges of the pan. Add the filling and then cover with the other crust and top with cubes of pancetta. Bake in the oven at 180° until the crust is golden.

THE LOCAL PRODUCT

PANCETTA PIACENTINA

The distinctive soft sweet flavour comes from the environmental conditions of the production areas (limited to areas no higher than 900 meters). The forest lands and temperate valleys allow for slowly and gradually seasoning the meat. It is best to take the pancetta out of the refrigerator an hour before cutting it because it is less tasty when it is cold. Pancetta is used plain as an appetizer with fava beans and pecorino cheese or cooked in a number of dishes to enrich the flavour and it blends well with many including legumes, first courses and even meat dishes.

MODERATE

AVERAGE

- 3 eggs;
- 200g grated parmesan;
- 300g breadcrumbs;
- 1 full litre of meat broth;
- 20g of beef marrow
- (or 25g of butter)
- nutmeg and salt to taste

Passatelli in brodo

Passatelli in broth

This famous recipe from Romagna was originally a very special dish for Easter lunch or important celebrations. There are a number of versions: with salami or ground beef, with spinach near Urbino and with lemon zest near Imola. Here you will find the basic classic and perfect recipe.

PREPARATION

Mix the parmesan, bread crumbs and egg until the mixture is dense. Add the beef marrow or butter (melted in a double boiler), the salt and the nutmeg. Knead the dough until it is very firm then form a dough ball and let the dough rest for one hour. Use a special passatelli maker or a potato ricer with large holes to make the passatelli pasta (with a diameter of around 3mm and a length of around 7cm). Boil the broth and cook the passatelli. The passsatelli are ready as soon as they float. Turn off the stove, wait a couple of minutes and serve.

THE LOCAL PRODUCT

GRANA PADANO

Grana Padano cheese was developed at the start of the year 1000 in the heart of lower Lombardy: the Cistercian monks from the Chiaravalle monastery developed the recipe as a way to preserve extra milk. Sources from the 12th century document the development of the first cheese factories for the production of a hard grainy cheese, which was named "grana", which means grain. It was very successful with the people of Lombardy and production developed rapidly. The long conservation favoured its sale to surrounding areas as well. The history of Grana continued through the centuries: it was used at the tables of amazing renaissance court banquets as well as during times of famine, when it contributed to supporting the country people. The production methods for Grana Padana have been handed down unchanged since then and still today the nutritional and organoleptic characteristics of this cheese endure making it one of the best loved and most imitated products in the world.

1 kilo of Bolognese sauce;
100g of grated parmesan;
500g of fresh lasagne
(or 400g if dry).

For the béchamel:
100g butter; 100g flour; 1 litre milk;
1 pinch nutmeg; salt to taste

Lasagna

Lasagne

This recipe and the ingredients are the embodiment of the richness of Bologna's traditional cuisine loved by all.

PREPARATION

For the béchamel: Melt the butter in a pan. Add the sifted flour and cook for a minute stirring constantly. Remove the pan from the stove and add the hot milk while stirring constantly. Place the pan back on the stove and cook over a low flame until the sauce boils, and then add salt and nutmeg. Cover the pan and cook the béchamel over a low flame for 15 minutes. Boil the fresh lasagne in salted water and a spoonful of oil (you can skip that if you are using dry lasagne). Butter the pan and cover the bottom with béchamel. Layer the pasta, béchamel, Bolognese sauce and grated parmesan to make five layers and top with a handful of grated parmesan. Bake at 200° covered in aluminium foil for 30 minutes and then remove the foil and cook for another 10 minutes.

THE LOCAL PRODUCT

EGG PASTA All rural communities in Italy have developed traditional dough and bread specialties. But how many can boast the absolute success of their inventions that have gone beyond local confines to tempt palates half way around the world. This is the case in Emilia and Romagna where they have been making dough for generations and handing down the secrets for the best-loved pasta and winning piadinas. Real Emilia pasta uses 1 egg per 100g of flour and only adds a little salt. Place the flour on a dough board and form a volcano shape with a hole at the centre. Break the eggs with a fork into the centre slowly and mix them into the flour and add salt. Now begin kneading by pressing and rolling it with the palm of your hand repeatedly for 10 minutes: it should be smooth without lumps. Roll out the dough with a rolling pin covered in flour and turn it frequently so that the dough is thin and uniform. It may be thicker or thinner depending on your preference and on the basis of what you want to make with the pasta.

Tagliatelle alla bolognese

400g tagliatelle pasta;
300g ground beef;
250ml meat broth;
150g pancetta;
50g carrot; 50g celery;
50g onion; 5 tablespoons of tomato sauce;
½ cup red wine;
20cl of whole milk;
pepper and salt to taste

Tagliatelle is one of the most well known and tastiest forms of pasta in Italian cuisine. Traditionally, this specialty is considered to have developed in the city of Bologna where tagliatelle are usually prepared with Bolognese sauce.

PREPARATION

Brown the diced onion, carrot and celery in the oil and butter. Finely dice the pancetta and after a few minutes add it to the pan with the ground beef and cook for a few minutes on a high flame. Add the red wine and cook until it evaporates (keeping the flame high) Add the tomato sauce (or concentrated tomato paste dissolved in a little broth), the broth, pepper and a pinch of salt. Cook (partially covered) for at least 2 hours mixing occasionally and adding the remaining broth and then the milk. After the sauce is complete cook the pasta in a large pan of salted water. Drain the pasta when it is al dente, place in a dish, cover with sauce and mix. Add grated parmesan and serve.

THE LOCAL PRODUCT

LAMBRUSCO
Lambrusco has ancient origins. In Latin it was called "labrusca vitis" and referred to a wild grape that grew at the sides of fields. Today the term is used to designate a group of grapes that are similar but not identical, which evolved over time to give rise to various wines including Sorbara with an unmistakeable lighter colour. It is produced in the Sorbara territory on the plains near Modena. A young and bubbly wine, it pairs well with the rich cuisine of Modena but it is also enjoyable as an appetizer or dessert wine.

TIME CONSUMING

AVERAGE

Tortelli di zucca

Squash tortelli

TIME CONSUMING | DIFFICULT

400 g flour; 1 whole egg and 1 yolk; 80g amaretto cookies; 1 full kilo of winter squash; 200g of parmesan; grated lemon zest; sage, butter and salt to taste.

It is very difficult to choose from the endless array of egg pasta varieties served in Emilia and Romagna. Instead of choosing the most famous, which have become part of Italian cuisine throughout the peninsula, we have chosen some of the lesser known with an intensely enjoyable flavour.

PREPARATION

Remove the seeds and bake the squash at 180° Celsius for 30 minutes. Peel the squash and the crust that has formed on the pulp and then squeeze out any extra liquid. Separately, mash the amaretto cookies and add them to the squash along with two-thirds of the parmesan. Mix and add the grated lemon zest and a little salt. In the meantime prepare the pasta with flour, eggs and water and knead until it is smooth and soft. Roll out the pasta dough (not too thin) and fold the sheet in half. On one side place small spoonfuls of the filling about 4-5 centimetres apart and then fold the other half over the top. Use a pasta cutter and cut into squares making sure that the edges have sealed well. In a pan melt the butter and chopped sage. Cook the tortelli in a large pan of salted water and drain after 5-6 minutes. Layer in a serving dish with melted butter and parmesan cheese.

THE LOCAL PRODUCT

PARMIGIANO REGGIANO

Parmigiano Reggiano cheese dates back eight centuries. Since that time the fragrance, production methods and areas of this world famous cheese have remained the same. There are references from the 11th and 12th century that prove Parmigiano Reggiano had the same characteristics then that it does now and they have become a legal quality standard. The fact that Parmigiano is an Italian classic is demonstrated by its presence in literature. The most important citation is by Boccaccio in the Decameron when he describes the land of Bengodi, he is able to make a mountain of grated Parmigiano appear under the reader's eyes writing something to the effect that "the people did nothing other than make macaroni and ravioli and once they were cooked, they rolled them in cheese to make them even tastier".

QUICK	EASY

Baccalà alla bolognese

Bolognese salted cod

800g of dried salted codfish (soaked and skinned);
2 grated garlic cloves; 1 lemon;
butter, extra virgin olive oil, parsley and pepper to taste.

THE LOCAL PRODUCT

BRISIGHELLA OIL

People have been cultivating olives around Brisighella longer than anyone can remember. During archaeological excavations in the 50s an ancient olive press from the second century BC was found just 4 KM from Brisighella. There are a number of references to large scale olive cultivation in this area in a number of historic documents, literary works and notary deeds from the 15th century forward. Some writings in the eighteen hundreds report a flowering processing industry (including olive processing).

While many of the dishes in Emilia Romagna are complex and articulate, the seafood dishes are absolutely essentialist. Though there are not as many unique seafood specialties, this simple recipe for salted cod is tasty and makes a great idea for a quick dinner.

PREPARATION

Cut the codfish into big chunks and rinse and dry them. Oil a pan and place the codfish covered in garlic, chopped parsley, oil, pepper and a few pats of butter. Cook over a high flame and lightly brown for around 6 minutes on each side taking care when you turn the pieces so that they do not break. Top with lemon and serve.

TIME CONSUMING

AVERAGE

Cotechino in galera

1 cotechino (500 g); 1 thick beefsteak large enough to encase the cotechino;
1 slice of ham (1cm thick); ½ an onion diced finely;
1 cup of white wine; 1 cup of meat broth; extra virgin olive oil, salt and pepper to taste.

Lots of people like cotechino served plain, but the Emilia Romagna region takes it one step further with this rich recipe that makes a great holiday dish.

PREPARATION

Boil the cotechino for around 15 minutes, drain and allow it to cool. Beat the beefsteak and add salt and pepper and cover it with the slice of prosciutto. Place the cotechino on top the steak and wrap the meat around it and tie it closed with kitchen twine. Brown the onion in oil, add the cotechino, the broth and the wine, then cover and simmer for around 40 minutes. Add broth and wine while cooking to keep the bottom from drying out. Cut into slices and serve with the sauce it was cooked in.

THE LOCAL PRODUCT

COTECHINO FROM MODENA

It is traditionally believed that Cotechino from Modena was created in 1511 in Mirandola. When the city was attacked by the troops of Pope Julius II, the townspeople had to find a way to preserve the pork so they started filling the pork rind with the meat and gave rise to Cotechino. It was so popular that by the end of the 1700s that Cotechino from Modena had replaced the famous yellow sausage that had made Modena famous in the Renaissance. Sale to nearby markets was favoured by the transformation of two local charcuterie shops into semi-industrial structures (Frigeri and Bellentani). From there the road was paved for Cotechino and by 1800 this product already had wide scale success.

Scaloppine all'aceto balsamico

Veal cutlets in balsamic vinegar

4 veal cutlets (bottom round or top round);
30g butter; 1 tablespoon of balsamic vinegar from Modena;
broth, flour and salt to taste.

MODERATE | AVERAGE

Veal cutlets in balsamic vinegar make a delightful second course that is quick and easy to prepare.

PREPARATION

Pound the cutlets to make them thinner and dip them gently in flour. Heat the butter and as soon as it begins to bubble place the cutlets in the pan. Brown the meat on both sides and add salt. Add a tablespoon of balsamic vinegar and cook until it evaporates. Slowly add a cup of broth as the liquid thickens. Serve the cutlets with the sauce they were cooked in.

THE LOCAL PRODUCT

BALSAMIC VINEGAR FROM MODENA
Differently than vinegar that is made from an alcoholic liquid, traditional balsamic vinegar is made from cooked grape must. The Romans used it as a concentrate (sapa) to flavour their food. Traditional balsamic vinegar from Reggio Emilia is linked to the land with a story that has lasted a millennium. The product was kept as a secretly guarded treasure until a few years ago and now it has become available commercially. Documents regarding its existence date back to the beginning of the last millennium. They say that the castle of Canossa produced vinegar, elixir and balsam that were much loved by the nobility. Historical documents from the 12th, 13th and 14th centuries mention the presence of consortiums of vinegar producers whose affiliates jealously guarded the secret of the precious product. The extensive dynasty that governed the duchy of Modena, Reggio and Massa up until Italian Unification enriched the chronicled memories about traditional balsamic vinegar. There are many references from the eighteen hundreds when it was quite standard practice to include vessels of balsamic vinegar and casks filled with the precious substance in the dowry of noblewomen.

FRIULI VENEZIA GIULIA

Aside from the excellent local products, the cuisine from this area is enhanced by a pleasant influence of varying tastes and traditions. We find an able blend of Slavic traditions and central European traditions dictated by the history of this land on the Italian border.

Polenta is used throughout the area – usually poured into a form, cooled and cut into slices to use as a base or a side dish. There are no lack of Austrian-Hungarian specialties like goulash or presniz (the traditional Easter dessert in Trieste) or Slovenian specialties like another very traditional dessert, Gubana (an Easter dessert in Gorizia which takes its name from the Slavic term "guba" meaning pocket - a pastry pocket stuffed with honey and dried fruit with a number of local variations in dough and filling).

Magnificent products come from the mountains and hills of the interior lands. Cheeses include the popular Montasio, l'Asìno, ricotta (plain or "cujncir" flavoured version); salamis include the unparalleled San Daniele prosciutto as well as the lesser known, but absolutely delicious musèt (a highly original cotechino made from pork face with lots of aromatic spices) and patina (ground goat meat salami mixed with lard, then dipped in corn flour, smoked and dried). There is a special tradition that is characteristic in Chiopris where goose is used fresh in many recipes and preserved foods. Lastly we cannot forget the fish dishes beginning with the trout (few wild trout, but lots of well-raised commercial trout) or the many seafood plates including brodetto, fish stew from the Adriatic Sea available in a number of different variations.

For dessert, the patisserie is refined with the use of mostly fruit (both dried and fresh) and the wonderful local honey. It is pointless to mention that the high quality wines and grappa perfectly highlight the great pleasure of Friulian dining.

WHERE TO FIND FRIULIAN SPECIALTIES IN ITALY

BOLOGNA	**PANE VINO E SAN DANIELE:** Via Altabella, 3/A - Tel.: 051 2960540 **L'ALTRO PANE VINO E SAN DANIELE:** Via Irnerio 10/A - Tel.: 051 4074218
GENOA	**OSTERIA PACETTI:** Via Borgo Incrociati 22/R - Tel.: 010 8392848
MILAN	**ALBERO FIORITO:** Via Andrea Pellizzone, 14 - Tel.: 02 70123425 **MANDI!! OSTERIA FRIULANA:** Via Nicola d'Apulia, 4 - Tel.: 338 1666817 **SAURIS & BORC DA BRIA:** Via Toselli, 2 - Tel.: 02 26825943
NAPLES	**PANE VINO E SAN DANIELE:** c/o Timecity Via Giordano, 17 - Tel.: 081 19579241
ROME	**PANE VINO E SAN DANIELE:** Piazza Mattei, 16 - Tel.: 06 6877147 **RISTORANTE IL TAJUT:** Via S. Giovanni in Laterano, 246 - Tel.: 349 6418088
TRIESTE	**BUFFET SIORA ROSA:** Piazza Attilio Hortis, 3 - Tel.: 040 301460 **LA TECIA:** Via San Nicolo, 10 - Tel.: 040 364322 **OSTERIA ALLA SCALETTA:** Via Donato Bramante, 4 - Tel.: 040 0642668
VENICE	**PANE VINO E SAN DANIELE RIALTO:** S. Polo 1544, Calle Botteri - Tel.: 380 4108446

Frico

250g of low fat cheese cut into ½ cm slices;
½ cup milk; 4 eggs;
100g butter; polenta and salt to taste.

A tasty appetizer that makes the most of Friuli's excellent cheeses for a perfect recipe. There are a number of different variations on frico (with apples, potatoes or bacon) but the element they share is that they are melted in the cheese.

PREPARATION

Cut the slices of cheese in squares around 5 centimetres per side; dip in milk and then in polenta. Heat 60g of butter in a pan and when it begins to boil, fry the slice of cheese until it is golden on both sides. In another pan heat the remaining butter and cook the eggs quickly; add salt and serve with the slices of fried cheese.

THE LOCAL PRODUCT

FRIULIAN WINES
Friulian wines have over two thousand years of documented history. Titus Livius wrote that it began when the Romans established the first colony in Agro Aquileiese in 180 BC. The production area with the Giulie Alps behind and the Adriatic Sea to the front extends across the hilly eastern strip of the province of Udine along the border with the Republic of Slovenia. The altitude varies between 100 and 350 meters above sea level with good climatic conditions and soil. It is produced in a wide range of types.

Jota

300g dry beans soaked for 12 hours;
200g of sauerkraut (canned is fine);
100g of polenta; 40g of lard (or prosciutto);
70g of butter; 1 cup of milk; 1 onion;
1 garlic clove; sage, parsley, salt and pepper to taste.

TIME CONSUMING

AVERAGE

This is a traditional farm dish and it was generally eaten as a single-course meal. It is common in Carnia and also in other areas with variations: in Carso we find barley and potatoes instead of the corn while in Trieste they eat a 'luxury' version with beef and pork ribs.

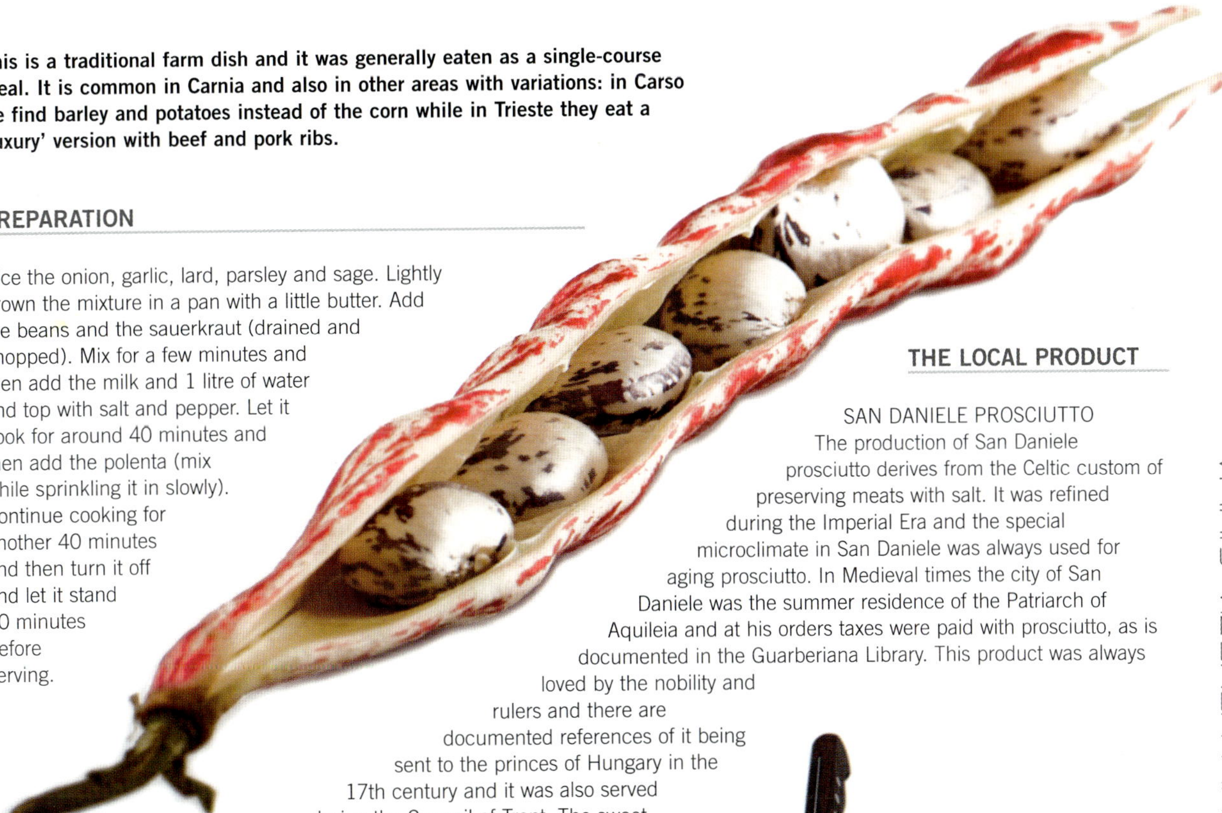

PREPARATION

Dice the onion, garlic, lard, parsley and sage. Lightly brown the mixture in a pan with a little butter. Add the beans and the sauerkraut (drained and chopped). Mix for a few minutes and then add the milk and 1 litre of water and top with salt and pepper. Let it cook for around 40 minutes and then add the polenta (mix while sprinkling it in slowly). Continue cooking for another 40 minutes and then turn it off and let it stand 10 minutes before serving.

THE LOCAL PRODUCT

SAN DANIELE PROSCIUTTO

The production of San Daniele prosciutto derives from the Celtic custom of preserving meats with salt. It was refined during the Imperial Era and the special microclimate in San Daniele was always used for aging prosciutto. In Medieval times the city of San Daniele was the summer residence of the Patriarch of Aquileia and at his orders taxes were paid with prosciutto, as is documented in the Guarberiana Library. This product was always loved by the nobility and rulers and there are documented references of it being sent to the princes of Hungary in the 17th century and it was also served during the Council of Trent. The sweet delicate prosciutto was so well liked by the refined palates of the Councillors that the magnificent town of San Daniele sent 30 pairs of ham on the back of a mule. It was also well liked by the refined princes and emperors of Austria and Hungary who chose the very best selections. Another famous enthusiast of this ham was Gabriele D'Annunzio who sent a friend from Brescia to Vittoriale to find some for him.

Paparot

TIME CONSUMING

AVERAGE

1 kilo of cleaned spinach; 100g of polenta or corn flour;
50g of wheat flour; 1 clove of garlic; 50g butter; 1 litre vegetable broth; salt and pepper to taste.

This is a traditional farm meal in the Carso area and it was a common dish during wintertime. There are a number of possible variations. You can use other vegetables in place of the spinach or even add eggs like they do in nearby Croatia.

PREPARATION

Cook the spinach without water (once it has wilted, drain and squeeze the spinach well and set the liquid aside) and chop the spinach. Heat the butter in a pan and brown the crushed garlic. After a few minutes remove the garlic and add the wheat flour, sifting it and mixing constantly. Allow the flour to toast for a couple of minutes, and then add the spinach and mix. Add the boiling broth and liquid from the spinach and bring to a boil. Slowly sprinkle in the polenta and continue mixing. Add salt and pepper and cook for about ½ hour.

THE LOCAL PRODUCT

MONTASIO CHEESE
There are three varieties that have been aged for varying lengths of time: fresco, mezzano and stravecchio. As the time it is aged increases, Montasio becomes more consistent and the soft delicate flavour becomes decisive, aromatic and sharp. It is great with fresh fruits and vegetables or as an ingredient in polenta or meat dishes or even grated over soups or pasta. Montasio has been made since 1200. The monks at the Abbey of Maggio Udinese developed the techniques for producing this cheese from those used in the high mountain pastures and the cheese took the name of the high Montasio plateau where the monastery once stood.

Baccalà alla cappuccina

700g dried codfish (soaked, skinned and deboned); 1 diced onion; 2 anchovies (cleaned and diced): 40g of each of the following: pine nuts and raisins that have been soaked in warm water; ½ litre of vegetable broth; half a piece of candied citron cut into slices; 1 cup of white wine; 1 teaspoon of sugar; 50g of grated bitter chocolate; 1 bay leaf; lemon zest, cinnamon, flour, breadcrumbs, extra virgin olive oil and salt to taste.

A very complex recipe with extraordinarily rich ingredients that give it an inimitable flavour. Here we find chocolate used in a very different way in Friuli. The mixture is best served atop slices of polenta.

PREPARATION

Brown the onion in a little oil. Cut the codfish into pieces, dip in flour and fry in a deep pan placing the pieces tightly side by side without leaving spaces. After a few minutes cover it with the browned onions and add the bay, anchovies, pine nuts, raisins, chocolate, lemon zest and a little salt and pepper. Cover it with boiling broth and allow it to cook over a very low flame for 3 hours (shake the pan occasionally to keep the codfish from sticking. Add more broth if needed. When the broth has absorbed add boiling wine, cover with breadcrumbs and bake in the oven at 200° Celsius until the top forms a crispy crust.

THE LOCAL PRODUCT

COLLIO GORIZIANO WINE (FORMERLY TOCAI)
Collio goriziano marks the confine between Italy and Slovenia with a chain of sunny soft and at times craggy hills that are protected by the Giulian Alpine foothills facing the Adriatic Sea which helps keep the climate mild. This land produces great wines that have been D.O.C. recognized since 1968 and that are made in a number of varieties. Tocai Friulano or Tocai Italico is a grape variety that is traditionally cultivated in the Friuli-Venezia Giulia region to make white wines that were sold under Geographic indications such as "Collio" or "Collio Goriziano". In 1993 the European Community and the Republic of Hungary signed an agreement to protect and control the names of wines. To protect the Hungarian geographic indication «Tokaj», the agreement prohibited the use of the term «Tokai» for the designation of the Italian wines mentioned as of 31 March 2007.

Brovade

TIME CONSUMING

AVERAGE

800g of cleaned white turnips;
1 onion thinly sliced;
50g of lard cut into chunks;
2 cloves of garlic; ½ litre of meat broth;
grape marc, salt and pepper to taste.

PREPARATION

Slice the turnips and place in a ceramic or glass container with alternating layers of grape marc. Allow the mixture to ferment for a few months: when the turnips turn an intense pink colour they are ready. Chop and gently brown oil, garlic, the diced turnips, salt and pepper and cook for a long time over a low flame adding broth as needed.

The climate of the mountain areas and the typical rural lifestyle leaves little room for waste giving rise to this wonderful way to preserve turnips, which are common throughout the region, and particularly in Carnia. It is a perfect accompaniment for pork dishes.

THE LOCAL PRODUCT

CARSO DOC: The production area goes from the high Carso plateau in the province of Trieste to the sea and even into the province of Gorizia. Carso is a high limestone plateau with a very arid soil. It is a difficult land that frequently feels the Bora wind which gives the wine its dynamic personality. The range includes various reds and whites derived mainly from Malvasia grapes (originally from Greece) and Terrano local Istrian grapes.

Gubana

TIME CONSUMING

DIFFICULT

For the dough: 600 g of general purpose flour; 30g of brewer's yeast; 2dl milk; 130g sugar; 100g butter; 1 lemon; 3 eggs; salt to taste.

For the filling: 150g walnuts; 100g raisins; 2 dry figs; 30g candied citron; 30g candied orange; 100g dark chocolate; 1 glass of Marsala; 2 tablespoons of breadcrumbs; 30g butter; 60g pine nuts; 2 prunes; 1 egg.

Gubana is a traditional speciality from the Natisone valley. It is generally served with a topping of Slivovitz, a liqueur made from distilled plums.

PREPARATION

Prepare the dough: heat 4 tablespoons of milk and when it has cooled add the yeast and stir until it dissolves. In a bowl, knead together 100g of flour, a level teaspoon of sugar and the brewer's yeast dissolved in milk. Knead until it forms a loaf and then cover it and allow it to rise. When it has doubled in volume, add the remaining flour and sugar, the egg, softened butter, a pinch of salt, grated lemon zest and milk until it reaches a soft and compact consistency. While the dough is rising prepare the filling: boil the walnuts, peel them and grind them finely with the pine nuts, figs, prunes and candied fruits. Put it all in a bowl and add the raisin (soaked in Marsala and drained) and the grated chocolate. Brown the bread crumbs in butter and add to the mixture, mix well and then add the egg yolks and the egg whites (beaten to form a meringue). Roll out the dough to form a thin rectangular sheet. Place the filling on the dough but leave space around the border. Roll the dough into a spiral (not too tight) and place it on a greased and floured baking sheet. Paint the surface with beaten egg yolk and top with sugar and bake at 190° Celsius for around 45 minutes. Serve cool or cold.

THE LOCAL PRODUCT

RAMANDOLO

The area of production in the Udine province is located in the hilly municipalities of Tarcento and Nimis (in fact the name of the product comes from a suburb of Nimis). Served at the Council of Trent in 1409, it is still produced exclusively with Verduzzo grapes, which are one of the oldest Friulian varieties. They are allowed to sun-dry on the plant or in special structures. The production is limited to 150,000 bottles per year. It is perfect with desserts, dry pastries and traditional desserts. It is also great with less common pairings such as elaborate and seasoned cheeses, prosciutto, cold cuts and smoked trout.

LAZIO

Artichokes are a true passion in Lazio and they have been for quite some time. Varro and Pliny the Elder both commented that Romans went wild over artichokes and they are used in a number of recipes. Roman-style artichokes are cooked whole and stuffed with garlic. Giudia-style artichokes originated in Rome's Jewish community - the golden fried artichokes are so well loved that they are a common Christmas Eve dinner treat. Artichokes are cultivated in a number of areas in the region including Ladispoli where they hold an important artichoke festival each spring. One particular local variety of artichoke is especially well loved. It is known as a "romanesca" or "mammola" and the artichoke is very tender with a round shape and it has no thorns. The artichoke that grows at the centre of the plant is the largest and it is referred to as the "cimarolo". Artichokes are also grown extensively in Sezze where they hold an artichoke festival in April.

The Romans have always had a passion for the sea and seafood and they have devised ingenious methods for cultivating it. Another common regional specialty is suckling lamb prepared in a number of ways, which tells the story of Rome's pastoral history. Roman cuisine also uses a number of scrap cuts of meat in a number of tasty specialties that are standards in local cuisine. Some of these scrap cuts include ox-tail, brains, intestine, tripe and sweetbreads all prepared masterfully.

A number of Roman specialties were imported from other places and then absorbed by the local culture. One such example is porchetta roasted pork, which is excellent in the Castelli Romani hills, but according to many the dish originated in Umbria. Pork is quite common in Roman cuisine and it always has been in fact there is even a road in Rome dedicated to it. Via Panisperna comes from the Latin terms "panis and perna" which mean bread and prosciutto.

WHERE TO FIND LAZIO SPECIALTIES IN ITALY

BOLOGNA	**AROMA DE ROMA:** Via Alessandrini, 19/D - Tel.: 051 247410
	QUANTO BASTA: Via del Pratello, 103/A - Tel.: 051 522100
MILAN	**GIULIO PANE E OJO:** Via Ludovico Muratori, 10 - Tel.: 02 5456189
	RISTORANTE RUGANTINO: Via dei Fabbri, 1 - Tel.: 02 89421404
	TAVERNA AI PARIOLI: Via F. Casati, 45 - Tel.: 02 67481919
NAPLES	**OSTERIA IL GARUM:** Piazza Monteoliveto, 2/A - Tel.: 081 5423228
PALERMO	**DA CALIGOLA:** Via Cusmano, 25 - Tel.: 091 6113284
ROME	**DA FERNANDO ER MATRICIANO:** Via Trionfale, 75 - Tel.: 06 39722466
	DA LUCIA: Vicolo del Mattonato, 2/B - Tel.: 06 5803601
	MATRICIANELLA: Via del Leone, 4 - Tel.: 06 6832100
TURIN	**RISTORANTE ROMOLETTO:** Piazza della Repubblica, 6 - Tel.: 011 5212269

Carciofi alla "Giudia"

Jewish style artichokes

MODERATE

EASY

6-8 cleaned Romanesque or Cimaroli artichokes (others varieties work fine as well); lots of extra virgin olive oil, salt and pepper to taste.

This is the most famous dish of the Roman Jewish community. The recipe owes its success to its simplicity, which highlights the qualities of the artichoke to the utmost.

THE LOCAL PRODUCT

ARTICHOKES

The word artichoke (and the Spanish, French and Italian term for artichoke) derives from the Arab word Harchiof or Alkharshuf which means ground thorn or sticker plant. The artichoke originated in Ethiopia where it was most likely bred from wild cardoons. In Lazio, the artichoke has been popular since Roman times and most likely it was also a common Etruscan specialty. Artichokes became popular throughout Italy in the 15th century and occupied a place of honour in culinary traditions until the later Renaissance. Artichokes are well suited to the climate and the soil and they are deeply rooted in the culinary traditions.

PREPARATION

Soak the artichokes in water and lemon for around ten minutes, drain and allow them to dry. Then beat the artichoke face down on a counter top to open the flower. Heat oil on a medium flame until it boils and then place the artichokes into the oil with the flower side down by holding them on the bottom of the pan with a fork until they are crispy. At this point, turn the artichokes upside down and let them cook until the heart is soft. Drain the artichokes and lay them on a paper towel to dry. Top with salt and pepper: they are best served piping hot.

Bucatini all'amatriciana

Amatrice-style bucatini

The meek lamb and the good pig together gave cheese and pork jowl... (C. Baccarà). These are the two simple ingredients that shepherds in Abruzzo would use to top their frugal yet substantial single course pasta meals. Amatrice is a smiling city in the Upper Sabina area, which is currently part of the province of Rieti. However in the past, it was part of Aquila, and therefore part of Abruzzo. This simple pastoral recipe developed into one of the most famous Italian specialties

500 g of bucatini pasta (type of thick spaghetti); 125 g of pork jowl; dry white wine; 6 or 7 San Marzano tomatoes or 400 g of canned tomatoes; one hot pepper; 100 g of grated pecorino cheese; extra-virgin olive oil; salt to taste.

PREPARATION

Put the oil, hot pepper and diced pork jowl in a skillet (preferably iron). Lightly brown the pork over a high flame and then add a little dry white wine. Remove the pork pieces from the skillet allowing them to drain well and set them aside (if possible put them in a warm place so that the pork remains soft and flavourful without becoming dry and salty). Remove the skin and seeds of the tomato (or drop them in boiling water for a moment to remove the skin more easily, and then cut them) and add to the pan. Add salt for flavour, mix and cook for a few minutes. Remove the hot pepper and return the pork to the pan and stir. In the meantime boil the pasta al dente in lots of salted water. Drain the pasta and put it in a bowl and add the grated pecorino cheese. Wait a few seconds and then pour in the sauce. Mix it all, and if you like, add more pecorino.

THE LOCAL PRODUCT

GUANCIALE PORK CHEEK This product has been prepared by farm families in the province as long as anyone can remember. The triangular pink intensely flavoured spicy and slightly smoked pork jowl is a kind of bacon. It is generally prepared at home or in small artisan shops. The pork cheek is trimmed into a rectangular shape and placed under salt for 4 or 5 days. Then the meat is then rinsed in white wine to remove the salt and then allowed to dry. After drying, the meat is sprinkled with pepper and red pepper and hung in a room with a fireplace (which gives it slight smoky hint). When the meat is absolutely dry, it is moved to the cellar to and aged for at least 90 days.

QUICK

EASY

Spaghetti alla carbonara
Spaghetti carbonara

QUICK

EASY

400 g of spaghetti pasta; 1 egg and 2 egg yolks; 120 g of pork jowl or unsmoked bacon cut into chunks; 150 g of grated pecorino romano cheese; extra virgin olive oil, salt and pepper to taste.

Traditionally rigatoni pasta is used but the recipe is also great with spaghetti or bucatini. In Italian a "carbonara" is a charcoal maker, and this dish owes its name to the men who worked at the charcoal pits in the forests that once surrounded the city. The ease of the dish, the use of ingredients that are easy to conserve and the heartiness of this dish fit perfectly in that scenario.

PREPARATION

Heat a large pan with water and salt to cook the pasta. In the meantime beat the egg yolks together with the pecorino cheese and a generous serving of pepper. Sauté the pork in a large pan with a little oil until the fat has become transparent and the meat is crispy. Cook the pasta al dente, drain and place it in the pan to cook for a couple of minutes at a high flame. Remove it from the stove, add the beaten eggs and mix quickly. Serve it with other grated cheese to be added at pleasure. There are different schools of thought on this dish: many people add a finely diced onion to the pork while others prefer garlic, and still others use both: you decide.

THE LOCAL PRODUCT

PECORINO ROMANO CHEESE

Few cheeses in the world have origins as old as Pecorino Romano, which was already being made in the first century AD when Latin agronomist Lucius Columella outlined the production process in "De Re Rustica". The ancient Romans used it as a condiment at Imperial banquets. The fact that it is long lasting and easy to digest made it one of the fundamental rations given to the soldiers of the Roman legions. These days most Pecorino Romano cheese in actually made in Sardinia. Due to growing demand for the product at the end of the 19th century, some of the larger cheese producers moved their operations to Sardinia (where sheepherding has always thrived) and knowledge of the process diffused locally. These days Pecorino Romano is still made with the same traditional methods – the curd is still cultured, coagulated and drained the same way.

TIME CONSUMING

AVERAGE

Rigatoni con la pajata

Rigatoni with “pajata”

400 g of rigatoni pasta; 800 g of “pajata” (suckling veal intestine or suckling lamb intestine); 50 g of bacon cut into pieces; 1 glass of dry white wine; 1/2 an onion, 1 carrot and 1 stalk of celery diced finely; 1 garlic clove; 1 clove; 500 g of tomato chunks or chopped boiled tomatoes; 80 g of grated pecorino romano cheese; 1 hot pepper; parsley (if desired); extra virgin olive oil, vinegar and salt to taste.

This is probably the most unique of all Roman specialties. It was born in Testaccio where it was prepared together with other scrap cuts for the employees of the slaughterhouse who were paid in part with these lesser cuts of meat.

PREPARATION

Skin the intestine (if you are able to find lamb intestine locally, the butcher may be able to do this for you) then rinse and place in a bowl and spray it with vinegar. After half an hour cut the intestine into 15-20 cm pieces. In the meantime prepare crushed garlic, onion, celery, carrot and unsmoked bacon and allow it to sauté in a large pan. After a few minutes add the intestine and let it cook until it has browned. Add the wine and cook until it has evaporated; then add the tomato, the clove, the hot pepper and the salt. Cook at low heat for around 3 hours (stir and add hot water if it becomes too dry). Cook the rigatoni al dente, drain and mix the pasta together quickly with the sauce. Then add pecorino romano cheese and, if you prefer, top it with parsley before serving.

THE LOCAL PRODUCT

VELLETRI WINE This wine is produced in the area surrounding the town of Velletri, in the zone south of the Castelli Romani area up to the countryside of Cisterna di Latina. It has always been a zone of high quality wine since the days of the ancient Romans. Pliny the Elder described the local production methods in detail. In the year 1500 it was the most popular wine in Rome. The white is ideal for appetizers, gnocchi alla romana, first courses with seafood, artichokes, roasted pork, omelettes and fresh cheeses. The red is a flexible wine that is suitable for the entire meal. The spumante versions are great for aperitifs or for accompanying delicate appetizers or the end of the meal.

Abbacchio scottadito

Crispy lamb ribs

1 kg of lamb ribs;
extra virgin olive oil, salt and pepper to taste.

QUICK | EASY

The excellence of simplicity: the success of this dish is all in the quality of the lamb (in Rome, suckling lamb is generally used). In Italian "scottadito" means 'burn your finger' because these tasty ribs are irresistible to eat with your fingers the moment they are removed from the flame ... which inevitably leads to the proverbial burnt finger.

PREPARATION

Flatten the ribs with a meat mallet, brush them with oil on both sides and add salt and pepper. If you like herbs you can also add a little tarragon. Cook them on a grill over a high flame (preferably over a charcoal fire) until they are crispy. You can also cook them on a very hot griddle for about 4 minutes per side. Serve with wedges of lemon as soon as they are ready.

THE LOCAL PRODUCT

ROMAN SUCKLING LAMB

"Abbacchio" is the Roman term for a suckling lamb. This ingredient plays a fundamental role in the history of cuisine in Rome and Lazio. The ancient Romans preferred kid goat to lamb (though Juvenal did write that suckling lamb was "the most tender of the flock – it has never tasted grass and is more full of milk than blood". Campo Vaccino was the animal market and in the 1400s it was the market for suckling lamb, lamb, wethers and ewes. Abbacchio was a common specialty from Easter to June when the one to six month old lambs were slaughtered. In the countryside during this time and also when the animals were sheared, the shepherds would eat 'pagliatella' or the meatier sections of the lamb intestine cooked over a fire and pieces of grilled meat known as 'pezzata' or 'sponsata'.

QUICK

EASY

8 small slices of veal cut finely;
4 slices of salt-cured ham (prosciutto crudo);
8 leaves of sage;
1/2 glass of dry white wine;
butter, flour, salt and pepper to taste.

Saltinbocca alla romana

Roman-style veal slices

The aroma of sage adds a touch of class to this simple and much-loved recipe.

PREPARATION

Place a leaf of sage and 1/2 a slice of ham on each cut of veal, attaching them with a toothpick. Bread the meat in the flour. Melt the butter in a pan and grill the meat at a high flame on both sides. Then top it with salt and pepper in the areas without ham. Remove the pan from the stove and the meat from the pan, take out the toothpicks and keep warm. Put the pan back on the stove and add wine and more butter to the drippings. Cook until it makes gravy and then pour it boiling hot over the meat.

THE LOCAL PRODUCT

PROSCIUTTO FROM BASSIANO
Bassiano is well known for preserving meat thanks to the climate and also for the local custom of making prosciutto. The pigs were kept in small raised pens for cleanliness. In the 60s local family processing began to be replaced by artisan-industrial processing with the development of agro-industries and a salami factory. This further extended the fame and the diffusion of the local product. The microclimate in the area is perfect - the humid winds from the plains meet the cool tramontana breeze here. The constant air flow ensures the ideal conditions for drying the meat.

Puntarelle

Catalogna chicory shoots

QUICK

EASY

700 g of Catalogna chicory shoots: washed, cut and "curled"; 1 garlic clove; 6 anchovies packed in oil; vinegar, extra virgin olive oil and salt to taste.

This wintery side dish is always present at Christmas Eve dinners. Catalogna is a special variety of chicory that is crispy and bitter. The leaves are removed one by one, washed and cut from the bottom to the point at which the stem is hollow on the inside. Then cut the stems lengthwise into small thin strips and place them in very cold water for 30 minutes (ice water is even better). This makes the puntarelle curl and eliminates the bitterness.

PREPARATION

Drain the puntarelle and let them dry. Use a mortar and pestle to grind the garlic and anchovies into a creamy paste; then add vinegar and oil and mix. Dress the puntarelle with the mix and add salt to taste.

THE LOCAL PRODUCT

CHICORY CATALOGNA FRASTAGLIATE FROM GAETA [PUNTARELLE]

This traditional vegetable has been planted in the fall for centuries to be eaten at Christmas and Easter. After the chicory is harvested, it is placed in wood or plastic crates. These days most people purchase the vegetable after it has been prepared. The light green stems are 40-50cm long. They differ from other kinds of chicory due to the long flower stems. The flavour is pleasantly bitter and the texture is tender and crunchy. The chicory stems are used to make "puntarelle". This requires peeling and cutting the long stems into small matchstick-size pieces that curl up when placed in cool water. They can be eaten with salt and lemon, added to salads or cooked.

MODERATE

EASY

Maritozzi

Traditionally a dessert served during Lent, the Maritozzo then became a typical breakfast sweet, without the addition of the traditional pine nuts. In many Roman cafes you can see them appetizingly displayed in their most tasty version: open and overflowing with lots of whipped cream.

500 g of raised bread dough; 20 g of pine nuts; 20 g of raisins; 3 tablespoons of powdered sugar; 3 tablespoons of extra virgin olive oil; orange zest to taste.

PREPARATION

Mix all of the ingredients together with the dough and quickly knead. Divide the dough into two small oval buns. Butter a baking pan and place the dough onto the pan without letting the buns touch. Let the dough raise until it has doubled in size. Bake in the oven at 200° for around 20 minutes. Before serving, dust with powdered sugar.

THE LOCAL PRODUCT

FRASCATI DOC

This is one of the oldest DOC wines and it has been recognised as a special typical product since 1933. Frascati is produced in the Castelli Romani hills near the municipalities of Frascati and the surrounding towns. The lands are of volcanic origin and they are rich in potassium, phosphorus and microelements which are permeable and dry. It is one of the oldest wine varieties and it filled the tables of ancient Romans back in the era of Tusculum's maximum splendour. It was made famous by Pope Paul III who used it at papal lunches. Exclusively white, it is produced in various varieties, which include the famous but rare Cannellino. It pairs well with appetizers, first or second courses of white meat or fish dishes, artichokes, omelettes, fried blue fish, vegetables and egg dishes. The dolce version is great to end a meal together with shortbread cookies or homemade desserts. The Cannellino variety pairs well with desserts like ricotta cake and the classic maritozzi.

LIGURIA

The fragrances and colours of Liguria are truly captivating with flowers cultivated for the entire European flower market, the aroma of basil, the marine air of the gulf, the resin of the pine tree canopy covering the coast and the forests climbing high into the Alps. We find a rich selection of pleasant aromas in the local cuisine as well thanks to the spices imported by Liguria's flourishing sea trade.

We begin with a basil variety with small intensely flavoured leaves that is native to Liguria. To make pesto (the region's most famous sauce) basil is ground with a mortar and pestle and mixed with other fine Ligurian products: very delicate olive oil from the hills and pine nuts produced by the awning of pines framing the coast. Pine nuts and garlic are used in a number of other meat and seafood recipes as well.

The most popular seafaring specialties in Liguria are based on less expensive varieties of fish such as anchovies and sardines (which are abundant in the gulf) eaten fresh or preserved for leaner moments or times when it was impossible to go out to sea. Masters at drying and salting fish, anchovies are an important ingredient in Liguria: they are eaten plain or used to enhance or flavour other dishes. Magnificent cultivated terraces built by the local farmers and nurtured by the mild climate give rise to an abundant harvest of vegetables and wild greens (including dandelion, wild chard, chicory, wild rucola, chervil and wild fennel) for natural salads or special fillings.

Meat is not a common item on local regional menus, but the few specialties are amazing. One example is Cima Ripiena, which is a veal pocket containing flavourful bay leaves, ground beef, sweetbreads, peas, mushrooms, marjoram, garlic, egg and parmesan cheese as well as the ever-present handful of pine nuts.

Among the many dessert specialties we find Panera: an ice cream dessert made with cream and coffee that has been pleasing refined Ligurian palates for over 150 years.

WHERE TO FIND LIGURIAN SPECIALTIES IN ITALY

FLORENCE	**IL PORCOSPINO:** Piazza Madonna Aldobrandini, 11 - Tel.: 055 217700 **PANE E OLIO:** Via Faentina, 2/R - Tel.: 055 488381
GENOA	**OMBRE ROSSE:** Vico Indoratori 20/24 - Tel.: 010 2757608 **TRATTORIA ANTOLA:** Piazza Manin, 16/R - Tel.: 010 871511 **TRATTORIA DELLA RAIBETTA:** Vico Caprettari, 10-12/R - Tel.: 010 2468877
MILAN	**LA TOPAIA:** Via Filippo Argelati, 40 - Tel.: 02 8373469 **OSTERIA VIA PRE':** Via Casale, 4 - Tel.: 366 1597478 **SAN FRUTTUOSO:** Viale Corsica, 3 - Tel.: 02 76110558
ROME	**TAVERNA GIULIA:** Vicolo dell'Oro, 23 - Tel.: 06 6869768
TURIN	**LA VIA DEL SALE:** Via S. Francesco da Paola, 2 - Tel.: 011 888389 **SAPORI DI MARE:** Corso Cosenza, 22/B - Tel.: 011 3174804

Cappunada

QUICK

EASY

80g hard tack (or unsalted hard crackers); 400g of tomatoes (red but not overripe); 200g of oil-packed tuna; 100g pitted black or green olives in brine; 50g botargo, tuna or mullet roe; 30g capers; 2 anchovy fillets; vinegar, extra virgin olive oil, salt and pepper to taste.

This traditional bread and tuna salad dish speaks of the seafaring people of Liguria. The hard tack (gallette in Italian) and all of the other ingredients (except tomatoes, which are a more recent addition to the recipe) were long-lasting foods that could be taken on long sea voyages.

PREPARATION

Wash the tomatoes, remove the seeds and cut into pieces. Drain the tuna and finely slice the botargo or roe. Rub the hard tack with garlic and moisten in with water and vinegar (not so much that it falls apart) and use it to line the bottom and sides of a large serving bowl. Cover with tuna, diced anchovy, botargo, tomatoes, capers and olives. Top with vinegar, salt and pepper. Mix and set aside for half an hour before serving.

THE LOCAL PRODUCT

TAGGIASCA OLIVES These plants were initially planted on property lines to serve as barriers and that is how they became an integral part of Liguria's famous terraced gardens. The first written reference to local Taggiasca comes from a colonial petition in 979 to lease lands "with the exclusion of olive groves". Later, Benedictine monks developed the olive variety with their tenacity and agricultural skill. In 1049 the monks received an olive grove from Countess Adelaide di Susa and the Taggiasca breed was developed on hillside terraces there with special agricultural methods. The variety was most likely developed with grafts and sets that were given to the monks by another group of Benedictines in Cassino. There is no doubt they did a good job since Taggiasca olives are still considered to be an excellent product. In the lands around Imperia and throughout Liguria, Taggiasca olives are used to make olive oil with a magnificent flavour: a fragrant delicate taste with a minimal level of acidity that makes it perfect for using fresh as a condiment or for cooking and enhancing even the most delicate flavours

Torta pasqualina

For the crust: 600g flour; 35ml oil; 350ml water; salt to taste.
For the filling: 1 kilo Swiss chard (or spinach); ½ an onion; 3 sprigs of marjoram; 130 g parmesan; 13 eggs; 500g ricotta; 1 cup of extra virgin olive oil; 1 dash of nutmeg; salt and pepper to taste.

TIME CONSUMING

AVERAGE

Torta Pasqualina savoury pie is a true Ligurian classic that is eaten and loved throughout Italy. Torta Pasqualina translates roughly as Easter Pie and it has been a specialty since the 1400s when it was strictly an Easter treat.

PREPARATION

Prepare the crust by mixing the flour, oil and water in a large bowl. Mix the ingredients well and then knead the dough by hand for a few minutes on a breadboard until it has a smooth texture. Divide the dough into 4 parts (2 larger parts around 330g and 2 smaller parts around 180g). Cover with plastic wrap and set it in a cool place for at least an hour. In the meantime prepare the filling. Boil the greens (add very little water), drain and squeeze to remove the excess liquid, then dice. In a skillet brown half a chopped onion in oil, add the greens and cook for a minute together with the onion to allow the flavours to blend. After the mixture has cooled, mix in a bowl together with 2 eggs, 50g of grated cheese, fresh chopped marjoram, salt and pepper; mix well. In another bowl mix the ricotta, 3 eggs, 30g of grated cheese, a dash of nutmeg and a pinch of salt. Mix well with a whip until the mixture is creamy and there are no lumps. At this point roll one of the larger pieces of dough into a very thin pie crust. Stretch it with your hands as you place it on a 30cm-diameter oiled pie pan. Gently press the crust up the sides of the pie pan and then brush the top of the crust with oil. Roll out the other large piece of dough and place it on top of the first and press it so that it adheres well. Add the mixture with the greens and gently press them to create a flat and level surface. Now add the ricotta and smooth it gently once again to create a flat level surface. Use the back of a spoon to create seven small indentions (one in the centre with six others surrounding it). Fill each indention with an egg yolk (be careful to not to break the yolk). Beat the egg whites and use them to cover the surface of the pie. Sprinkle with 30g of parmesan. Roll out one of the smaller crusts and use it to cover the top of the pie (make sure that it attaches to the lip of the pie pan. Brush the surface with a little oil and roll out the other crust and place it on top (making sure that it attaches well). Use a knife to cut off any excess crust and fold the edges inwards to create a border and press to seal the crusts together. Brush the surface with a little oil and bake in a pre-heated oven at 180° Celsius for 45 minutes.

THE LOCAL PRODUCT

COLLINE DI LEVANTO WINE
The vineyards grow along the coast between Sestri Levante and Portovenere. The local soil has a high clay and limestone content in this hilly interior land dotted with greenery and small towns. The wine takes its name from the municipality of Levanto, which has a magnificent climate and environment and works actively to promote the local territory. The white pairs amazingly well with seafaring specialties including appetizers and seafood while the red accompanies vegetarian dishes and white meats excellently.

Ravioli in salsa di noci

Ravioli in walnut sauce

500g flour; 4 eggs; 200g of each of the following ingredients rinsed and cut into small strips: spinach, Swiss chard and borage; 100g sheep-milk ricotta; 100g brains and sweetbreads; 1garlic clove; 8 walnut halves; 300g pine nuts; 80g grated parmesan; powdered nutmeg, extra virgin olive oil, butter and salt to taste.

TIME CONSUMING

DIFFICULT

Pesto is not the only Ligurian sauce specialty. This walnut sauce is less common, but it makes a great topping. The ravioli have a rich and especially tasty filling. Even though the dish is somewhat laborious, the results are well worth the effort.

PREPARATION

Mix the flour with 3 eggs, a little salt and warm water and knead to form a smooth dough. Cover and set aside for half an hour before rolling out two very thin sheets of pasta dough. Boil the brains and sweetbreads in a pan of salted water and then brown in a pan with a little butter and salt (mixing constantly). After around 7-8 minutes remove the pan from the stove and mash the ingredients with a fork. In the mean time boil the vegetables for a couple of minutes, drain and squeeze them to remove any excess moisture and then chop very finely to create a paste. In a bowl mix the vegetable paste, 1 egg, ricotta, the mashed brains and sweetbreads, very finely diced garlic and a dash of nutmeg. Mix well until it forms a smooth spread. Take a sheet of the pasta and place small spoonfuls of the mixture on top of it (each spoonful should be about 7 centimetres apart). Lay the other sheet of pasta on top and use your fingers to press the dough around the spoonfuls of filling. Cut the pasta into ravioli with a pasta cutter and lay on a large tray covered in flour. Prepare the walnut sauce separately. Grind the walnuts, pine nuts and garlic together with a mortar and pestle. Boil the ravioli in a pan of salted water and drain after a couple of minutes. Lay the ravioli on a warmed serving dish and cover with walnut sauce, grated parmesan and serve.

THE LOCAL PRODUCT

RIVIERA LIGURE EXTRA VIRGIN OLIVE OIL

Taggiasca olives are harvested by 30 January each year. They are gathered by hand or through a process called "battitura", which is performed with a device that gently shakes the olive branches so that the olives fall from the trees onto large nets without ever touching the ground. The olives are then cold pressed with old-fashioned traditional granite presses in order to maintain the fragrance, flavour and nutritional qualities of the olive. Riviera Ligure olive oil is great for topping any dish and its flavour is never overpowering. The delicate flavour makes it perfect for appetizers, first and second courses and even pastries.

Spaghetti al pesto

QUICK | EASY

400g trofie pasta; 50g basil; 2 garlic cloves; 75g pine nuts; 50g grated pecorino cheese; 50g grated parmesan; extra virgin olive oil, salt to taste.

Pesto is the classic symbol of Genoa – some say this fresh uncooked sauce is even an aphrodisiac.

PREPARATION

Use a mortar and pestle or blender to grind the garlic and pine nuts while slowly adding the basil and salt. When the mixture is smooth add the pecorino cheese and oil to form a dense sauce. Cook the pasta in a pan of salted water and drain when the pasta is al dente. Top with parmesan and a couple spoonfuls of the water used to cook the pasta; then add the pesto. Mix well and serve.

THE LOCAL PRODUCT

PESTO ALLA GENOVESE

The most famous sauce in the region is pesto without a doubt. The main ingredient is basil and the name pesto comes from the method used to make the sauce (in Italian 'pestare' means to grind or crush). This is an essential process and it makes the flavour of the ingredients come alive. There are two secrets to making great pesto. Use basil leaves from young plants (no older than 2 months old). Ligurian farmers know this and they have developed special farming techniques to provide a fresh supply at all times. You should also crush the basil and garlic with a mortar and pestle instead of using the quicker blender method – it takes a little longer by hand but you really can taste the difference. To make true Genoese pesto sauce the only ingredients are basil, garlic, extra virgin olive oil, pine nuts, salt and cheese (preferably parmesan or pecorino).

Buridda

TIME CONSUMING

AVERAGE

800g cleaned fish of your choice (monkfish, conger, cuttlefish, octopus); 3 anchovy fillets;
40g of dry mushrooms soaked in warm water; 2 ripe juicy tomatoes (sliced with the seeds removed);
1 garlic clove; 1 carrot and 1 stalk of celery; 1 onion; flour, parsley, extra virgin olive oil and salt to taste.

Fish braised in an aromatic flavourful sauce. One unique aspect of Ligurian cuisine is that mushrooms are used in lots of specialties including seafood dishes.

PREPARATION

Dice the garlic, onion, carrot, celery and parsley stems and brown in olive oil. Add the anchovy fillets and mash into pieces with a wooden spoon. Add the seafood and a pinch of salt and continue browning for a minute and then add the diced mushrooms and tomatoes and simmer in a covered pan over a low flame. The fish should be cooked in 10 minutes but the octopus and cuttlefish require more time. When the seafood is ready and the sauce has thickened, top with diced parsley leaves and serve.

THE LOCAL PRODUCT

MONTEROSSO SALTED ANCHOVIES

Anchovies from the area that runs between Sestri Levante and La Spezia are medium sized with a lovely balanced taste (due to the level of salinity there) that is flavourful but delicate. The anchovies spawn from the middle of June to the end of July when the water temperature rises and creates a perfect nursery for propagating the species. Anchovies are referred to as "pisces salsi" in documents written during Medieval times in a number of local town charters and deeds. In Monterosso we find documents that outline the phases of the anchovy salting process during the 17th century. The fish were cleaned and then loaded into wood barrels or terracotta vases with salt for 20 days before they were sold. The containers were kept in "caneva" or cellars and in 1646 there were at least six in the Monterosso area.

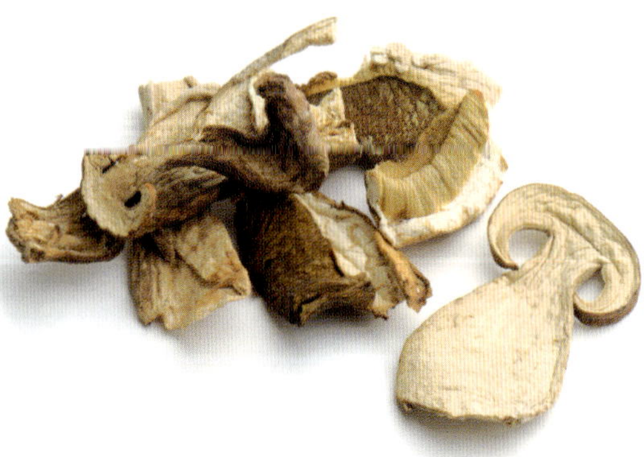

Cappon magro

4 slices of hard tack; 200g cauliflower; 200g green beans; 2 carrots and 1 stalk of celery; 2 potatoes, 2 artichokes; 1 beet; 2 garlic cloves; 1 fish weighing around 800g (sea bass, umbrine or hake) cleaned and deboned; 1 small lobster; 10 scampi or large shrimp; 4 oysters or 12 mussels (cleaned); 100g of mushrooms packed in oil; 1 soft bread bun; 2 anchovy fillets; the juice of 1 lemon; 30g capers; parsley, red pepper, extra virgin olive oil, vinegar and salt to taste.

This seafood delight is a truly sumptuous and beautiful dish that is overflowing with flavour – an absolute culinary triumph.

PREPARATION

Moisten the bread with water and vinegar. In the meantime dice 1 garlic clove, parsley, the spicy red pepper and capers. Squeeze any excess moisture from the bread and mix it with the diced mixture. Continue mixing while you very slowly pour in 1 cup of oil. Clean the vegetables and boil them in salted water as follows: in one pan place the cauliflower, green beans, celery and carrots and in another pan place the potatoes, artichokes and beets. Boil the fish and crustaceans separately in another pan and then cut the fish into chunks and peel the crustaceans. Top the fish with oil, salt and lemon juice. Rub the hard tack with garlic, moisten with water and vinegar and top with a little oil. Place the hard tack on the bottom of a serving dish. Cover with alternating layers of fish, crustaceans and vegetables. Cover each layer with a little of the diced mixture and oil. Finish with the crustaceans, mushrooms, oysters and mussels (open the oysters and mussels over a flame and remove the shells).

THE LOCAL PRODUCT

QUARANTINA BIANCA GENOVESE

Potatoes reached the Liguria region at the end of the seventeen hundreds thanks to agronomists and wise parish priests who foresaw that this tuber could be a valid replacement for grain in times of famine. And, after a poor harvest that was unable to satisfy the peoples' needs, hunger made this vegetable into an important staple. The Quarantina Bianca Genovese is the most popular local variety grown in the mountains surrounding Genoa. Despite the name (quarantina refers to the short 40-day period) the variety is a semi-early bearer, it maintains well and is well-suited to the sandy mountain soil. With an excellent flavour, it is great for all sorts of specialties including gnocchi potato dumplings, stockfish stew or even added to pasta with pesto sauce.

Seppie a zemino

Cuttlefish a zemino

1 kilo of cleaned cuttlefish, rinsed and cut into strips; 400g of Swiss chard cleaned and parboiled; 1 clove garlic; 2 celery stalks; 20g dry mushrooms soaked in warm water; 20g pine nuts; 1 tablespoon flour; extra virgin olive oil, salt and pepper to taste

In Liguria and nearby Tuscany, the term "zemino or zimino" is used to refer to a mix of diced browned herbs and vegetables that generally contains chopped Swiss chard. In contrast to the similar Tuscan dish, this cuttlefish specialty uses a mushroom and pine nut sauce instead of tomato sauce.

PREPARATION

Drain the cuttlefish, lay on a paper towel to dry and then brown in oil together with diced garlic, celery and a little salt. Dice the Swiss chard and add it to the mixture. After 15 minutes add the sliced mushrooms, pine nuts (ground in a mortar and pestle), flour and a little warm water. Cook in a covered pan over a low flame for 45 minutes. Cook until the sauce reaches the desired thickness and serve a couple of minutes after removing from the stove.

THE LOCAL PRODUCT

WHITE GARLIC FROM VESSALICO The distinctive trait of this breed of garlic is that it is very long lasting with a delicate aroma, an intense flavour and a little spiciness. The heads of garlic are pulled from the ground at the end of June and allowed to dry without removing the long stems. Then they are arranged by size and the stems are woven together during the morning or the evening when the air is more humid. Usually each braid holds 25 garlic heads though these days braids of 13 are becoming more common due to the decrease in average family consumption. This product has an ancient history in the land and a local garlic fair has been held annually since the seventeen hundreds (it is held every year on 2 July) by decree (the Liber Decretorum decree is kept at the Vessalico municipal building). Local cuisine celebrates the qualities of garlic with "ajè" sauce which is basically mayonnaise and garlic (the recipe calls for one clove per egg yolk – though the ratio is usually a little less in more contemporary versions) commonly served with boiled potatoes with the skins on.

MODERATE

DIFFICULT

Pan dolce genovese

400g flour; 20g brewer's yeast; 60g butter; 100g sugar; 1 teaspoon of orange flower extract; ½ cup Marsala wine; 5g fennel seeds; 20g pistachio nuts; 20g pine nuts; 40g raisins; 40g citron; 40g candied orange; milk and salt to taste.

This sweetbread recipe is Liguria's most famous classic Christmas specialty. It is made from long-lasting foods like dried fruits and nuts, which are common in many local winter recipes. The fennel seed and orange flower extract give the dish a delightful aroma.

PREPARATION

Dissolve the yeast in warm water and add it to part of the flour and allow it to rise for a few hours. Then add the rest of the flour, the melted butter, Marsala wine and orange flour extract. Mix well and add the other ingredients. Form a round loaf, cover it with dish towel and let it rise for a couple of hours. Cut an X on the surface of the bread and bake at 200° Celsius for around 1 hour. It is best if it is allowed to cool before serving.

THE LOCAL PRODUCT

CINQUE TERRE WINE

This wine takes its name from the Ligurian Riviera where it is produced (it is also produced on a hilly strip of land in the province of La Spezia). The vineyards are cultivated along a rocky coastal ridge with compact rocky soil. Over the centuries this arid land has been turned into thriving terraces. The morphology of the land makes it impossible to gather the grapes any other way than by hand making the wine even more special. This wine was loved by many famous Italian writers including Boccaccio, Petrarch and D'Annunzio. It pairs perfectly with saltwater and fresh water fish, seafood and flavourful cheeses. The Sciacchetrà version is a dessert wine for dunking biscotti and accompanying traditional desserts or flavourful cheeses.

LOMBARDY

This fertile and industrious land is graced by bountiful high quality cuisine thanks to the morphology of the landscape and the many different kinds of production areas. If we explore dining traditions in Lombardy we find ourselves tracing a map of territorial flavours: traditional mountain specialties from the alps and alpine foothills, food from the lowlands or the fertile Padana valley and incredible selections from the soft rolling hill lands and large lake areas.

We find tasty rice and risotto dishes (inspired by the fantastic local kinds of rice including Vialone, Nano and Carnaroli), fine polenta (made from local Pavese Mais del Re corn) incredible dairy products (from the magnificent valley pastures and plains like Grana Padano) as well as excellent wine and olive oil from the lake areas.

Each tiny area has a rich variety of flavour-filled sensations. In Pavia we find a very popular goose meat salami and in the Sondrio province Violino di Capra (goat prosciutto) is an unusual local treat while the local bresaola (dried, salted beef) is popular all over Italy. The selection of cheese is rich and the Valtelline Valley is famous for Casera and Bitto cheeses. Pizzocheri (a rustic kind of pasta made from buckwheat flour) is another local favourite. Cremona specialties include a scrumptious mostarda (similar to chutney) and excellent salami. In Mantua they make mostarda from apples and the recipe is a little different but just as delicious. Near Brescia we find Cuz della Valcamonica (a lamb meat spread conserved in terracotta jars) as well as local sheep-milk cheeses like the famous Bagoss. There are a number of fine cow milk cheeses in the Bergamo area as well (Taleggio, Gorgonzola and Quartirolo), while Lodi is famous for the magnificent Pannerone.

In Milan we find all of the regional specialties at restaurants and local specialty stores. Milan also creates its own interpretations of regional dishes. Just consider Risotto alla Milanese, Costolette alla Milanese or Ossobuco alla Milanese, which are known throughout the country. The most famous Christmas treat in Italy is Panettone and they have been making them in Milan since Medieval times.

WHERE TO FIND LOMBARDY SPECIALTIES IN ITALY

GENOA	**TRATTORIA LOMBARDA:** Via Finocchiaro Aprile, 26 - Tel.: 010 594629
MILAN	**ANTICA OSTERIA IL RONCHETTINO:** Via Lelio Basso, 9 - Tel.: 02 8262762 **EL BARBAPEDANA:** Corso Cristoforo Colombo, 7 - Tel.: 02 8321732 **OSTERIA DEL COMUNE ANTICO:** Via Comune Antico, 62 - Tel.: 02 6425323
ROME	**RISTORANTE VELANDO:** Borgo Vittorio, 26 - Tel.: 348 8137047

Casonsei

TIME CONSUMING

AVERAGE

300g flour; 100g beef (boiled and diced); 120g diced salami; 1 egg; 1 garlic clove; 1pear (mashed in the blender); 1 tablespoon of breadcrumbs; 80g butter; 60g grated grana padana cheese; sage, nutmeg, cinnamon, milk and salt to taste.

Casonei stuffed pasta shells are prepared in a number of different ways and the pasta dough is sometimes made with egg. The recipe below is the way it is prepared in Bergamo where they use an eggless pasta dough, which is the more traditional recipe.

PREPARATION

Mix the flour, salt and a little warm water and knead until it forms a smooth firm dough. Cover and set aside. In a mixing bowl, mix together the beef, salami, garlic, grated breadcrumbs, egg, half of the cheese and the whipped pear. Mix well and add a little salt, cinnamon and nutmeg (if the dough is too stiff, add a little milk). Roll out the dough into a thin sheet and cut out disks (8cm in diameter) with a pasta cutter. At the centre of each disk place a spoonful of the filling and fold the disk in half (wet the edges and fold them over with your fingers to seal them well). Boil the casonei in a large pot of salted water (remember that eggless pasta takes a little longer to cook). Drain the pasta and place in a serving dish and top with melted butter, sage and the rest of the cheese.

THE LOCAL PRODUCT

SALAMI FROM LOMBARDY

They have been making salami from Lombardy since the days of the Lombard invasion. After discovering an Alpine valley with a perfect climate for producing and aging salami, the Lombards launched an economic program aimed to support local pig farming and salami production, which contributed to consolidating the local consumption of pork. The monastic orders also furthered the development of charcuterie processing methods for health and medical reasons. Salami from Varzi was very popular with the Marquis Malaspina, the local landowners who invented and produced it for their own family consumption. Later, merchants would travel the salt trading routes throughout Europe with this popular salami.

Pizzoccheri

TIME CONSUMING

AVERAGE

350g buckwheat flour; 100g of wheat flour;
500g cleaned Savoy cabbage; 300g butter;
300g fresh cheese (Casera or Valtellina if possible);
3 garlic cloves; 100g grated Grana Padana or parmesan cheese; salt to taste.

One of the basic staples in the local rural cuisine (beyond rice and polenta) has always been buckwheat, especially in the mountains. This very famous recipe comes from the Valtelline area and it calls for the local Casera cheese. The original recipe for this buckwheat flour pasta contained loads of butter (even more than this one) but it was intended to feed people who had been outside in the cold wind doing hard labour all day long. Adjust the recipe to fit your lifestyle.

PREPARATION

Mix the two kinds of flour and a little warm water together. Knead the dough until it has a velvety texture. Roll out the pasta dough into sheets (around 3-4 millimetres thick) and cut it into strips (about 7 centimetres long). Bundle the strips together and cut them into 1½ centimetre lengths. Melt the butter in a pan with crushed garlic cloves and then set it aside. In the meantime, drop the cabbage (chopped into large chunks) into a pan of boiling water. After 5 minutes add salt and the pasta. Let the pasta boil for 8-10 minutes. Remove part of the cabbage and pasta from the pan and place in a deep serving dish. Cover with grated cheese and slices of fresh cheese then continue layering with cabbage and a layer of pasta and repeat. At the end top with the melted butter and garlic and serve in ceramic bowls that have been heated.

THE LOCAL PRODUCT

VALTELLINA CASERA CHEESE

This semi-fat soft cheese is made from the whole milk of local breeds of cows that feed on wild pasture grasses. The recipe calls for the milk from two or more milkings. Then the milk is partially skimmed and coagulated. The cheese has a cylindrical shape with a compact straw yellow crust that becomes more intense in colour as it ages. It has a mild flavour with a delicate hint of nuttiness that also becomes more intense as it ages. Valtellina Casera cheese is a tasty and delicate addition to summer salads and many other recipes. It is great by itself (especially if it is aged and accompanied by a glass of red wine). It is an essential ingredient in many of the traditional recipes of Lombardy including Pizzocheri buckwheat past, Sciatt (buckwheat and cheese fritters) and Taroz (a cheesy potato and green bean dish).

Polenta taragna

350g buckwheat flour;
250g polenta corn flour;
600g Fontina cheese
(or Casera or Bitto);
700g butter;
3 litres water;
salt to taste.

MODERATE

EASY

Polenta Taranga is a specialty of Valtelline and the valleys surrounding Brescia and Bergamo. It is prepared with a mixture of buckwheat and polenta flour which is mixed with a large helping of butter and fat or semi-fat cheese right before serving.

PREPARATION

Use a copper polenta pan (or a steel pan with a thick bottom) and fill it with salted water and add one third of the butter. Bring the ingredients to a boil and then sprinkle in the corn flour and the buckwheat flour while stirring constantly in order to avoid lumps. Mix the polenta constantly and cook for around 50-60 minutes. In the meantime cut the remaining butter and cheese into chunks. When the polenta has finished cooking, lower the flame and add the cheese and butter. Mix until the cheese and butter have melted and mixed into the polenta.

THE LOCAL PRODUCT

BITTO CHEESE
The origin of Bitto cheese dates back to the era when the Celts settled in the Sondrio province valleys. The Celtic word "bitu" (perennial) was given to the valley and the stream that crosses it as well as the delicious cheese made there. The production techniques for making Bitto are still substantially the same as those used by the ancient Celts. For centuries, bitto was used as currency to pay the rent on pastureland. These days there are around 70 alpine farms that are still specialised in producing Bitto. The transhumance (seasonal movement of livestock) to the alpine meadows lasts for a canonical 84 days. Strictly traditional techniques are used to make the cheese and therefore the organoleptic qualities have remained intact making the specialty a timeless favourite of those living in the Valtelline valley. In 1908 Bitto producers launched their first initiative to protect and promote the local product by founding the Società dei caricatori d'Alpi di Morbegno.

QUICK

AVERAGE

Risotto allo zafferano

Saffron Risotto

400g Arborio or Vialone rice; 50g of beef marrow; 1 onion; 20 saffron threads; 1.5 litres meat broth; 100g butter; 100g grated cheese

Saffron risotto is a traditional specialty in Lombardy. This golden risotto is made in a number of different ways according to many different recipes and it is prepared by chefs all over the world. Common variations on saffron risotto include the addition of mushrooms (porcini if possible), sausage or even scampi and other types of seafood.

PREPARATION

Finely slice the onion and brown it over a low flame in the butter and crumbled marrow. Cook for around 10 minutes stirring constantly. In the meantime place the saffron threads in a bowl and pour ½ litre of boiling broth over the top. Remove the onion from the pan and pour the rice in and brown it for a few minutes mixing well with a wooden spoon. Add two ladles of broth and stir. Cover the sauce pan with a lid and allow the rice to absorb the broth. Continue adding broth two ladles at a time until the rice has finished cooking (about 20 minutes). Remove the pan from the flame, mix the rice with the remaining butter and half of the cheese and stir. Wait a couple of minutes before serving.

THE LOCAL PRODUCT

SFORZATO DI VALTELLINA WINE

This is a rare and very unique wine that is produced on the hilly banks of the Adda river surrounded by large steep mountains covered in garden terraces at a height of 700 metres above sea level where the vineyards thrive. It is believed that the Ligurians were the first people to terrace these sunny lands and make them arable. The wine is made from Nebbiolo grapes that are selected and dried on screens for around 110 days until the sugar content reaches the point that it will raise the alcohol level to 15 percent. It pairs well with red meats and aged flavourful cheeses - a great wine that commands respect and contemplation.

Cassoeula

200g pork rind; 2 pork feet; 500g of pork short ribs; 2 pork ears; 2 pork tails; Luganega (lean, mild pork sausage); 500g pork spare ribs; 1 glass white wine; 2 Verzini (sweet pork sausages); 1 Savoy cabbage; 1 carrot and 1 stalk of celery; 1 onion; 40g butter; 1 litre vegetable broth; extra virgin olive oil to taste.

Cassoeula is a hearty traditional winter meat dish in Milan and Lombardy. It is said that Arturo Toscanini went wild for Cassoeula. These days it is both a winter and summer specialty served at many local town festivals in Lombardy.

PREPARATION

Boil the ears, feet, pork rind and pork tails for about 45 minutes in a large pan of water then drain and cut the meat into pieces. In a skillet brown the spare ribs and short ribs for around 10 minutes in a little butter. Then in another pan brown the Luganega sausages cut into pieces with the Verzini salamis. In another pan cook the cabbage (do not add any water, but the leaves should be wet) until the leaves have wilted. Use a very large pan to brown the chopped carrot, celery and onion. Then add the Luganega and the Verzini and a glass of wine (cook until the wine evaporates). Add a little broth and cook for 10 minutes. At this point add the rest of the meat and cook for another 5 minutes before adding the cabbage. Mix well, cover and cook over a low flame adding broth only if necessary.

THE LOCAL PRODUCT

SALAME DI VARZI

Salame di Varzi is made from fresh pork from pigs raised with traditional techniques with a live weight of at least 150 kilos at the time of slaughter. The cuts used include the shoulder, thigh, loin, fillet, neck, belly and top quality ground pork. When it is consumed, the product is marked with a special seal only if it is tender to cut and has a bright red colour with a perfectly compact grain and the right proportion of perfectly white lard. The flavour is sweet and delicate and it has a characteristic aroma from the seasoning process. The salami is traditionally cut into rather thick slices and it is said that the slice is the right size when it can stand on edge without falling over. It pairs well with olives and vegetables packed in oil used as traditional Italian appetizers. However it is also great with cheeses and hard-boiled eggs. It should be accompanied by full-bodied red wines or younger novella and Beaujolais wines.

TIME CONSUMING

AVERAGE

MODERATE

AVERAGE

Costolette alla milanese

4 veal chops with bone; 2 eggs; 100g butter; 1 lemon; breadcrumbs and salt to taste.

These veal chops are representative of Lombardy and the local culinary tendency to brown things in butter slowly over a low flame and the fine quality of the meats (those raised in Brianza are especially good). This recipe is now a common specialty throughout Italy, though it is rarely prepared according to the original recipe.

PREPARATION

Pound the meat flat and make a couple of cuts on the backside so that the chops do not curl up when cooking. Beat the eggs and dip the chops in the egg without dipping in "the handle" (the bone tip). Then dip it in breadcrumbs and press the breadcrumbs with your hands so that they attach well. Heat the butter in a pan (do not allow it to fry) and add the veal. Cook over a medium flame on both sides until golden brown. Place the meat on a serving plate and garnish with lemon slices to squeeze onto the meat after serving.

THE LOCAL PRODUCT

RIVIERA DEL GARDA BRESCIANO WINE
The grapes grow on the western banks of Garda Lake in around thirty municipalities in the province of Brescia in the same area as the DOC certified Garda wine. The wines are available in a number of varieties. The reds are ideal with roasted, braised and grilled meats or game. The Chiaretto is perfect with appetizers and white meats; the Novello makes a great aperitif and accompanies delicate flavours or snacks; the rosè spumanti is a great dinner wine. Groppello is a perfect pair for chicken, grilled meats, salami and cheeses while the white is excellent with freshwater fish and crustaceans.

TIME CONSUMING

DIFFICULT

Ossobuco alla milanese

4 cross-cut veal shanks (sliced 2-3 centimetres thick); 100g butter;
chopped mixture A: diced carrot, onion, celery stalk, 1 garlic clove, marjoram and lemon zest; 1 cup of meat broth;
chopped mixture B: 1 garlic clove, lemon zest (or mixed orange and lemon zest); 200g of tomato sauce;
1 glass of dry white wine; flour, salt and pepper to taste.

This braised veal is an excellent dish and its popularity is well deserved. It does require a little time but the results are amazing and it makes a perfect holiday dinner. In Milan they use the sauce to top risotto served as a side dish.

PREPARATION

Flour the veal shanks. Melt part of the butter in a pan and brown the meat on both sides. Add salt and pepper and top the meat with the chopped mixture "A". Allow it to cook a few minutes before adding the wine then continue cooking until the wine evaporates almost entirely. Then add the tomato sauce and broth, cover and cook over a low flame for at least 1 hour. Top with chopped mixture "B" and the rest of the butter, mix for a few minutes, remove from the stove and serve.

THE LOCAL PRODUCT

TERRE DI FRANCIACORTA WINE
The production area is located in the southern part of Franciacorta on the soft hills between Bergamo and Brescia to the south of Iseo Lake near Mt. Orfano, which has an especially temperate microclimate. It is one of the seven areas where Franciacorta is produced: with higher highs and lows, a great solar exposition and a unique limestone soil, the wine is completely unique. The whites are great for an aperitif and they accompany fish and rice dishes well. The reds pair best with hearty first courses and braised or boiled meat dishes, kebabs and ossobuco alla milanese.

MODERATE

EASY

DESSERT

Torta sbrisolona

Sbrisolona cake

2 egg yolks; 200g butter; 150g polenta corn flour; 250g all purpose flour; 200g sugar; 150g blanched almonds and 50g of natural almonds; 1 vanilla sachet; the zest of 1 lemon

Sbrisolona is a crumbly cake that was invented by poorer farmers. However, with the passage of time richer ingredients were added to satisfy the palates of the rich populace of Mantua.

PREPARATION

Chop the almonds (not too finely) and set aside one handful of whole almonds (with the skin) for topping the dessert. In a large bowl mix together all of the ingredients: both types of flour, the blanched almonds, butter, vanilla, lemon zest, two egg yolks and sugar (set aside two tablespoons of sugar). Mix the ingredients together quickly (do not knead the mixture or form a compact dough). Butter a cake pan (at least 25 cm in diameter) and sprinkle the dough in the pan (crumble it with your hands as much as possible). Then top the cake with the almonds you set aside and bake at 180° Celsius for around one hour. Allow the cake to cool and remove it from the pan. Top the sbrisolona cake with the rest of the sugar and serve.

THE LOCAL PRODUCT

MOSCATO DI SCANZO WINE This may be one of the DOC wines in Italy with the smallest production quantities but it has a long history and is quite prestigious. The production area is limited to the municipality of Scanzorosciate, which is one of the largest in the Bergamo province. It is located in the hilly lands on the left bank of the Serio River and runs all the way to the Alpine foothills of Bergamo. Moscato di Scanzo is made from carefully selected native grape varieties that probably reached the area following Roman colonization. The wine is complex and suited to contemplation. It is a delight by itself or paired with desserts or sharp cheeses.

MARCHE

The cuisine of this region contains a storehouse of specialties created through the expert ability and dedication that distinguishes the region. The pork specialties are highlights with two different and contrasting types of salami that are both exquisite: the very popular spreadable Ciauscolo is made from scrap cuts of meat, while the more noble cuts are used to make Salami from Fabriano. Ciauscolo is soft and spreadable and flavoured with lots of garlic, pepper, nutmeg and white wine. Salami from Fabriano is almost completely lean so it undergoes a process called "larding" where bits of lard are added to the filling) and it is only flavoured with salt and pepper. This is also another place that is famous for roasted pork. In the Marche region it is most famous in Monterado where they have been holding a festival in its honour during the middle of May for almost half a century. The Region is also famous for its high quality beef which is produced in large quantities and sold all over Italy. The animals are allowed to graze out in the open and you can definitely taste the difference in the meat. The lands in the Marche region also produce rich truffles: the black and white truffles from Acqualagna are famous. In Acqualagna, truffles are the basis of the local economy. The town has a local council dedicated to them and they hold three truffle festivals each year: one during the second half of February, one on August fifteenth, and one between October and November. In Sant'Agata Feltria they hold the Italian national truffle festival, which involves all of the areas where truffles grow in central Italy, from the middle of October to the middle of November.

The fish dishes are also great with "brodetto" fish stew from the Adriatic sea and the "Garagoi" molluscs (which are abundant along the coast) cooked in an aromatic sauce of tomatoes, oil, wine and herbs. The desserts are also unusual and refined. In a letter in 1826, Leopardi asked his father to save some "Marche figs" referring to the traditional Lonzino di Fichi: a dessert of sun-dried figs, anise, almonds and walnuts that is dipped in rum or Mistrà (a dry anisetto). The rose hip cream is also a must the preparation is complex but the flavourful outcome is worth it – frequently served with local chesses.

WHERE TO FIND MARCHIGIAN SPECIALTIES IN ITALY

ANCONA

OSTERIA DELLA PIAZZA: Piazza Ugo Bassi 14/B - Tel.: 071 2814235
TRATTORIA DELL'ANTIQUARIO: Via Flaminia, 69 - Tel.: 071 2141286
TRATTORIA LA MORETTA: Piazza Plebiscito, 52 - Tel.: 071 202317

MILAN

DA STEFANO IL MARCHIGIANO: Via A. G. Edoardo, 1 - Tel.: 02 33001863

ROME

AL CEPPO: Via Panama, 2 - Tel.: 06 8551379
DA CHECCO E LINA: Via Cesare Paoletti, 25/27 - Tel.: 06 8411237
RISTORANTE MARIANO: Via Piemonte, 79 - Tel.: 06 4745256

Olive ascolane

400g of large green olives (Ascolane olives are perfect); 100g of each of the following ground meats: beef, chicken, pork; 1 chicken liver;
50g grated cheese;
2 eggs; grated zest of 1 lemon; a few spoonfuls of breadcrumbs soaked in broth;
4 tablespoons of tomato sauce; onion, celery, carrot, cloves, grated breadcrumbs, flour, extra virgin olive oil, salt, pepper and nutmeg to taste

Stuffing and frying olives is a laborious task indeed, but they make a delicious appetizer that is a true sensation of culinary imagination. Unfortunately this specialty is frequently sold as a prepared food that generally turns out to be a somewhat deluding guesstimate.

PREPARATION

Pit the olives (or cut them off the pit: be careful to maintain the olive whole). Prepare the filling. Brown the meats and herbs and spices, then add the tomato sauce and cook until it thickens. At this point remove the spices and mix in all the other ingredients adding the cheese, lemon zest, 1 beaten egg, a pinch of nutmeg and some of the breadcrumbs. Fill the olives and dip them in beaten egg and then in breadcrumbs before deep-frying.

THE LOCAL PRODUCT

OLIVA ASCOLANA FROM PICENO
Local history says that Rossino and Puccini loved Ascolana olives in brine. In earlier times, the olives from Piceno were served in the Roman Imperial cafeterias. Ascolana olives are as large as almonds and they are especially soft due to the kind of soil they grow in: loose and deep with a prevalence of limestone. As the name says, these olives originated in the Ascoli Piceno province and also a large part of Teramo in the area between the Tronto and Vomano rivers.
These incredibly tender olives have a delicate flavour, lots of pulp and particularly fine skin. They are known best for the most popular recipe: stuffed, fried Olive Ascolane.

TIME CONSUMING

AVERAGE

MODERATE

AVERAGE

Brodetto di pesce

800g of fish, molluscs and mixed crustaceans (catch of the day),
1 glass of vinegar or white wine; 200g tomato sauce;
onion, salt and pepper (or hot red pepper) to taste

This famous fish stew is the boast of the sea in the Marche region. However, it is hard to pin down the authentic recipe because there are numerous versions that all claim to be the "real" Marchigian Brodetto. This version is one of the most popular.

PREPARATION

Clean the fish. Finely slice the onion and brown it in a little oil. When the onion turns golden in colour add the tomato, 1 cup of vinegar or white wine, 3 cups of water, salt and pepper (or hot pepper) and let it boil for a few minutes. Then add the fish (begin with the largest pieces that take the longest time to cook and gradually add the others on the basis of their cooking time). Continue to simmer until all of the seafood has finished cooking and serve. You need to be careful to not overcook or undercook the seafood and that requires a little familiarity with the various cooking times required for different kinds of seafood.

THE LOCAL PRODUCT

VERDICCHIO DI MATELICA WINE
These grapes are grown in the Esine Valley in an area that runs along the Apennine chain between the province of Ancona and Macerata and the heart of the production area is the city of Matelica. The grapes are cultivated along a hilly strip of land between 400 and 650 meters in altitude with a total production area that is no larger than 270 hectares. The wine is well suited to a number of dishes but it is best with seafaring specialties. It pairs well with rice, soup, white meats and charcuterie specialties.

TIME CONSUMING

AVERAGE

Vincisgrassi

600g egg pasta; 1 litre béchamel sauce; 150g grated parmesan; 50g butter; 20g breadcrumbs; salt and nutmeg to taste. For the sauce: 300g ground beef; 600g of lean beef and pork tips;
1 sausage or a slice of well-chopped pancetta (70/80g); chicken gristle and nerbetti (gristle and sinew usually used for soup stock); one section of oxtail; one tube of tomato concentrate; 400g of thick tomato sauce;
2 onions; 1 celery stalk and 1 carrot; 1 glass of white wine; 3 or 4 cloves; marjoram, salt and pepper, olive oil and a pat of butter.

An oven-baked pasta dish, "vincisgrassi" owes its name to Prince Windisch-Graetz who was very enthusiastic about it in 1799 when he led the Austrian Army to tear Ancona away from Napoleon's troops.

PREPARATION

Prepare a ragout sauce the day before (it needs to simmer for a long time – at least three hours). Then in a large pan brown the well-diced onion, the crumbled sausage or bacon and brown it in a little oil and a pat of butter. When the onion turns golden in colour add the ground beef and continue browning. When the meat has browned, add the beef and pork tips, the chicken giblets (well cleaned and cut into pieces) and the oxtail. Continue to cook and add a dash of white wine. Finely dice the onion, celery and carrot and add it to the mixture. Mix and add the rest of the wine. Dilute the tomato concentrate with water and add it to the pan. Add the cloves, marjoram, salt and pepper and bring the mixture back up to a boil and add the nerbetti. Add the tomato sauce. Now the sauce needs to simmer delicately for a long time so lower the flame. Allow it to sit over night. For the pasta: Roll out a very fine sheet of dough. Cut it into rectangles around 20 x 10cm. Cook the pasta in boiling salted water (two or three at a time). Cool in cold salted water and lay the pasta on a smooth white cloth to dry. Butter the pan and cover it with a thin layer of béchamel sauce, then a layer of ragout and then sprinkle it with parmesan. Continue layering to form 5 to 12 layers (as you prefer). The dish is usually served with the béchamel and parmesan layer on top. Add a few curls of butter and top with breadcrumbs and bake at 180° Celsius for 30 to 40 minutes.

THE LOCAL PRODUCT

WHITE VEAL FROM THE CENTRAL APPENINES
The meat comes from purebred Chianina, Marchigiana and Romagnola cows and bulls between 1 to 2 years old. The animals are raised in pastures until they have finished suckling. Afterwards they are fed with fresh or dried forage from natural and cultivated fields in the area or with simple or compound concentrated feeds with the addition of vitamins and minerals. The meat is sold with a label indicating Vitellone Bianco dell'Appennino Centrale and the IGP certification is embossed on the outside of 18 different cuts of meat.

Stoccafisso all'anconetana

Ancona-style Stockfish

MODERATE

AVERAGE

850g of dried soaked stockfish; 4 anchovy fillets; 300g potatoes (peeled and cut into chunks); 500g of tomato chunks; onion, marjoram, extra virgin olive oil, milk, salt and pepper to taste.

This recipe for creamy stockfish is both flavourful and delicate thanks to the unusual milk base.

PREPARATION

Brown the onion, marjoram and diced anchovies in oil. Then add the tomato chunks, a little salt and pepper and cook over a low flame for half an hour. Place the pieces of stockfish in a large deep pan together with the sauce and a little oil and surround the fish with the potatoes. Then top it with milk. Cover the pan and boil for about 5 minutes, then place the pan in the oven and cook at 180° Celsius until the sauce has thickened adequately.

THE LOCAL PRODUCT

ROSSO CONERO WINE

This wine is produced in the south-eastern section of Ancona in the Monte Conero area it is named for. This promontory is detached from the lower ridge of the Appenines at a height of 572 metres projecting out into the Adriatic Sea. The origins of the wine date back to medieval times when a Benedictine monastery produced a famous red wine from grapes harvested on the slopes of Mt. Conero. The wine accompanies the hearty flavours of local Marchigian cuisine. The younger wines pair well with Ancona-style stockfish, salami and flavourful succulent dishes in general. The aged wine pairs well with stuffed pasta and first courses with meat sauce, roasts and braised meats, game and flavourful cheese (especially pecorino di fossa cheese).

Triglie alla griglia
Grilled Mullet

QUICK

EASY

4 mullet (red mullet is best) weighing 150g each; extra virgin olive oil, bay, salt, pepper and lemon to taste.

This is a simple classic dish – the most important factor is the freshness of the mullet.

PREPARATION

Clean the mullet and make a few small cuts on both sides. Prepare a marinade with oil, salt, pepper, chopped bay leaves and marinate the mullet for about an hour. In the meantime prepare the charcoal and then grill the mullet (turning occasionally and brushing it with marinade). Serve steaming hot with slices of lemon.

THE LOCAL PRODUCT

OFFIDA DOC WINE

This wine is produced on the hills around Piceno between the Aso and Tronto Rivers in an area that is equidistant from the sea and the mountains. The heart of the wine country is the ancient town of Offida, for which the DOC wine is named. There are two white wines (Pecorino and Passerina) made from native grapes that were rediscovered recently as well as a red and a vin santo. The whites pair best with fish, crustaceans and seafood. The red blends with stronger flavours such as roasted or grilled red meats and aged cheeses while the Passito is great at the end of the dinner with dry cookies or strong cheeses.

MODERATE

AVERAGE

Bostrengo

400g rice; 200g sugar (or honey or Sapa); 2 eggs; grated lemon and orange zest; 150g of raisins and pine nuts; 150g of grated dark chocolate; 2 or 3 tablespoons of very strong espresso; 100g of dried chopped figs; rum or Alkermes liqueur to taste.

This dessert is full of unexpected flavours and it makes a tasty and robust end to any meal.

PREPARATION

Cook the rice in salted water (or milk) until it is al dente. In the meantime mix all of the other ingredients and heat them over a low flame for a few minutes. Add the rice and mix well. Place the mixture in a baking pan and bake for around an hour at 180° Celsius. When the surface is golden in colour, remove the pan from the oven and allow the cake to cool. Top with powdered sugar before serving.

THE LOCAL PRODUCT

SAPA Sapa is a syrupy natural sweetener that was used much like honey in past times when sugar was expensive and hard to obtain. It also added a special flavour to foods and beverages. It was prepared at home when the grapes were harvested. The ripest grapes were selected, crushed and allowed to ferment for one day. The grapes were then pressed and filtered and the must was placed into a large copper pan (on three legs with a fire built beneath it to cook slowly for a long time until it thickened into syrup). Four litres of juice made one litre of sapa. The sourness and acidity of the sapa was moderated by dipping homemade white bread into it. It was flavoured with grated lemon peels. In order to keep the precious syrup from attaching to the bottom of the pan, they added a few unshelled walnuts. The sapa was then poured into wooden barrels to cool and deposit any sediment. The next day it was bottled and then kept in the pantry or cantina. Sapa is used In a number of ways: to top beans, chick peas, chestnuts; in fine desserts, in the filling of tortelli stuffed pasta shells; to flavour polenta and in cakes, sweetbreads and even candy.

MOLISE

Molise has been separate from Abruzzo for quite some time, but we cannot really say the same thing about the local cuisines which are really quite similar. In both regions we find maccheroni alla chitarra (looks like square spaghetti) as a local favourite. There are a number of creative pasta specialties and the pasta is almost always just durum semolina and water as tradition commands. Some of the favourite forms include strozzapreti, taccozzelle, cirioli, fusilli, cavatelli, calcioni and lasagnelle... During his famous trip to Italy at the end of the 1700s, Goethe was amazed at the variety and quality of the pasta in Molise. Another similarity with Abruzzo is the use of large or even massive quantities of spicy red pepper which is locally referred to as "Lazzariello".

Along the drover's road that connected Pascasseroli with the Puglia plains, which was vital for the shepherding industry in the area, Molise developed and elaborated what is referred to as "cucina di tratturo" or drover's cuisine, which used a lot of lamb and kid goat, as well as wild boar and pigeons that were hunted while the herds grazed. The intensity of livestock farming in the area also gave rise to a number of cheese specialties (scamorze, burrini, trecce, caciocavalli, pecorini and the famous cheeses of Agnone). Pigs are also raised and there are a number of local varieties of charcuterie specialties made including Salami from Guilmi, a number of local varieties of Ventricina, magnificent Soppressata and many different varieties of sausages and salamis almost always flavoured with and preserved under fat.

More recently truffles and oil have also been cultivated to produce fine products (especially around Larino). The town holds two tasting festivals in the middle of December: one in Larino, "the new oil Festival" and one in Roccavivara known as "Panunto". Both festivals are dedicated to the new oil, which is tasted atop traditional bread and many other specialties.

The coast is also important to local flavours with a number of soups and recipes for mullet and sea bass that enrich the cuisine. Walnuts and almonds are also cultivated and the confectionary industry is important locally.

WHERE TO FIND MOLISAN SPECIALTIES IN ITALY

CAMPOBASSO

LA GROTTA DI ZI' CONCETTA: Via Larino, 7 - Tel.: 0874 311378
TRATTORIA IERI E OGGI: Via Trieste, 17 - Tel.: 0874 1951857
VECCHIA TRATTORIA DA TONINO: Corso Vittorio Emanuele, 8 - Tel.: 0874 415200

ROME

KING DEI MOLISANI: Viale Angelico, 41 - Tel.: 06 37514772
LE VOLPI DEL MOLISE: Via Alberto da Giussano, 37 - Tel.: 06 21700759
RISTORANTE LA CASCINA: Via di Boccea, 903 - Tel.: 06 61905528

Calcioni molisani

Molise-style Calcioni pasta

300g flour; 3 eggs; 1 lemon; 300g sheep-milk ricotta; 80g of each of the following: ham and sharp provolone cheese cut into chunks; parsley, extra virgin olive oil, salt and pepper to taste.

MODERATE

EASY

This is a popular and tasty local version of fried stuffed pasta shells.

PREPARATION

Start by preparing the filling: blend the ricotta, 1 egg, diced parsley, cheese and ham chunks and a dash of salt and pepper in a mixing bowl. The mixture should be firm to the touch. Set aside for half an hour. In the meantime prepare the pasta: form the flour into a volcano shape with an indention at the centre. Break the eggs into the indention, add a little salt and knead the dough until it is smooth (add a little warm water if it is too dry). Roll out a thin sheet of pasta dough and fold it in half. Place spoonfuls of the filling on one half of the pasta sheet and fold the other half over the top. Use a pasta cutter to cut out the calcioni (taking care to seal the edges well first). Deep fry a few at a time in oil until they turn a lovely golden brown.

THE LOCAL PRODUCT

CACIOCAVALLO AND RICOTTA CHEESE

Two products stand out in the list of dairy specialties from Molise: the caciocavallo cheese from Agnone and the ricotta cheese from Pietracatella. Caciocavallo from Agnone is made from fragrant milk that comes from free-ranging cows raised on the mountains. There are two versions: the more delicate version uses veal rennet while the more flavourful variety uses goat rennet. After cooking the curd is processed by hand and formed into a classic pear shape. The cheeses are tied in pairs and hung in cool airy places to age for around four months. Ricotta from Pietracatella has been made the same way for centuries and is a symbol of local identity. The farmers each bring their own milk and then they process the cheese all together in a sort of bonding ritual. Another sign of the importance and significance of the product is that Santa Maria di Costantinopoli (the most popular in the community) is affectionately referred to as "Santa Maria della Ricotta".

MODERATE

AVERAGE

Cavatelli incatenati

400g durum semolina flour; 100g pancetta;
1 cup of extra virgin olive oil;
4 eggs; salt and pepper to taste.

THE LOCAL PRODUCT

PENTRO D'ISERNIA WINE

The wine is produced in two distinct areas. One of the areas is the valley north of the Verrino River and the other is in the countryside around the city of Isernia. The vineyards are planted on hills with a good exposition and an altitude no higher than 500-600 meters. The name of this DOC certified wine comes from the Pentri populace "people of the mountains" who lived in these lands in Ancient times and were the most important branch of the Samnite civilization. The white pairs perfectly with cheeses and light first courses. The red is suited to first courses topped with meat sauces or meats and flavourful cheeses. The rosé is a perfect accompaniment for beans, eggs, salami and game.

There are several types of Cavatelli pasta in southern Italy, but the Molisan version is unique. It has a small shape and it has no egg in the pasta dough. This recipe uses cavatelli pasta to make a sort of carbonara.

PREPARATION

Mix the flour with warm water and a little salt and knead it into a firm and elastic dough. Set aside in a covered bowl for around 1 hour. Make tubes of pasta (about 20 cm long) and then cut them into 2 centimetre pieces. Press the pieces in the centre with the point of your index finger. Boil the cavatelli pasta in a pan of boiling salted water and cook al dente. In the meantime brown the diced bacon in a well oiled pan and add the drained cavatelli pasta. Mix the beaten egg and top with salt and pepper: mix until the eggs become thick and make the cavatelli stick together.

SECOND COURSES

Calamari farciti

Stuffed squid

1 kilo of cleaned squid;
2 anchovy fillets;
2 garlic cloves; 1 teaspoon of capers; parsley,
breadcrumbs, dry white wine, extra virgin olive oil, salt and pepper to taste

MODERATE

AVERAGE

This delicious recipe is a specialty in Molise as well as nearby Puglia. The version from Molise has a more intense flavour with the addition of anchovies and capers in the filling.

PREPARATION

Dice the squid tentacles, anchovies, garlic, capers and parsley then add breadcrumbs and oil. Add a few spoonfuls of water (or tomato sauce) until the filling has a dense and creamy consistency. Use this mixture to fill each calamari three-fourths full and then close it with a toothpick. Place the calamari in a pan with a little oil and brown before adding a dash of wine, water, salt and pepper. Continue cooking over a medium flame until the calamari is tender (use a fork to test the consistency) and the sauce has thickened.

THE LOCAL PRODUCT

BIFERNO DOC

The production area is located in the low valley of the Biferno River, from which this DOC certified wine takes its name. The area runs from Campobasso to the Adriatic Sea and the vineyards are cultivated on hills on both sides of the river. The white pairs best with mozzarella, caciocavallo cheese and trout. The red is great with oven-roasted white meats or grilled red meats, flavourful salamis and cheeses as well as soppressata and rabbit cacciatore.

TIME CONSUMING

AVERAGE

Salsiccia ai semi di finocchio con fagioli

Sausage with fennel seed and beans

8 medium-size sausages; 300g dried cannellini beans; 450g of tomato sauce; 2 onions, 1 celery stalk and 3 or 4 cloves of garlic; bay, rosemary, fennel seed and red pepper, extra virgin olive oil and salt to taste.

This is a very hearty second course for winter evenings and a pleasant dinner in front of the fireplace.

PREPARATION

After soaking the dry beans for at least 8 hours, drain them and then boil them in salted water and a couple of cloves of garlic (leave the skin on). After the beans have finished cooking (they should be soft but not mushy), remove the garlic and rosemary and leave the beans in the liquid. In the meantime, use a fork to poke holes in the sausage and brown it over a low flame in a pan covered with lots of fennel seeds and red pepper. After browning for fifteen minutes on each side, remove the sausage from the pan and keep warm. Add a little oil to the sausage drippings and gently brown the onion, garlic, celery and a bay leaf. Add the tomato sauce and salt and hot pepper. Cook over a medium flame for ten minutes. At this point add the beans (drained) and the sausages, mix together and cook for another 10 minutes.

THE LOCAL PRODUCT

PORK LIVER SAUSAGE

This sausage is filled with one part of lean pork, one part of soft fat and a third meat (pork liver, heart, lung or red meats). The meat is all ground together with ten millimetre screw blades and then stuffed into natural casing and tied. The sausage is allowed to dry for a few days in the kitchen and if it is not consumed immediately it is covered with lard, which makes it very long lasting.

Peperoni ripieni

Stuffed bell peppers

4 large yellow or red peppers;
6 anchovy fillets;
200g breadcrumbs;
100g tomato sauce;
red pepper powder,
extra virgin olive oil and salt to taste.

MODERATE

EASY

Though it may not be light, it is certainly very tasty. The cuisine in Molise aims to please without lots of complications. To make a simple dinner, combine this hearty side dish with a fresh, light second course.

PREPARATION

Wash the peppers, deseed and remove the veins. Toast the breadcrumbs for a couple of minutes in oil, then add the anchovies and diced parsley, salt and hot red pepper and a few tablespoons of oil. Mix together and use this mixture to stuff the peppers. Then place the peppers in an oiled baking pan and top with salt, oil and hot pepper and tomato sauce diluted in a little water. Bake in the oven at 180° for around 50 minutes (baste the peppers with the sauce while they are baking).

THE LOCAL PRODUCT

OIL FROM MOLISE The fame and notoriety of oil from Molise has been documented by a number of different authors throughout the ages. During the Imperial Era, it was praised by Columella in his treatise "De Re Rustica" and by Plinius in "De Oleo" and by Horace in his Satires. Even Cicero praises the hard work of the people of Larino and the fertility of their land in "Pro Cluentio". The land is very well suited for olive cultivation and over the years certain varieties grew more popular such as the Aurina, Gentile di Larino, Rosciola and black olives from Colletorto, which are loved throughout the territory and are closely linked to the geographic areas where they are grown. In later eras, the oil from Molise was mentioned in the writings of a scholar from Salento in 1700 named Giovanni Presta who wrote that in past times it was reserved for the most delicate, exigent and richest palates.

DESSERT

QUICK

EASY

Crespelle

200g flour; 2 eggs; 40g butter;
40g sugar; extra virgin olive oil, vanilla sugar,
grated lemon zest and salt to taste.

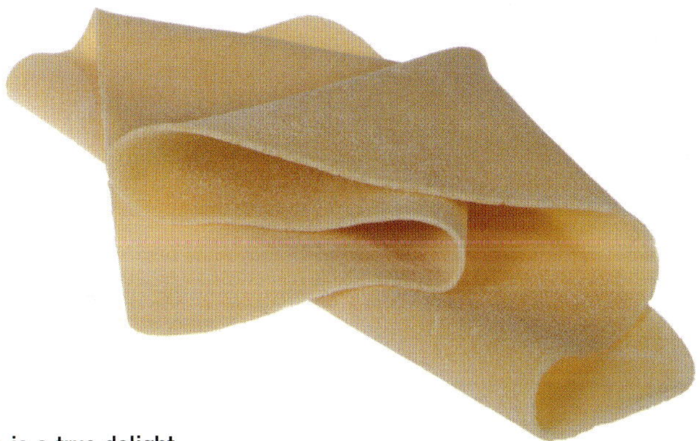

These simple fritters require few ingredients and are easy to prepare but the sweet crispy treat with a hint of lemon is a true delight.

PREPARATION

Mix the flour, eggs, sugar, room-temperature butter, a pinch of salt and lemon zest (you can substitute the lemon zest with ½ cup of vino cotto). Roll out a thick sheet of dough and cut out shapes as you please. Deep fry the dough in oil a few at a time. Use a slotted spoon to remove the fritters when they are golden brown and place them on paper towels to absorb any extra oil. Top with vanilla sugar and serve.

THE LOCAL PRODUCT

MOLISE DOC WINE
This DOC certified wine is made throughout the region in 70 municipalities. Molise is almost entirely made up of hills and mountains and it is good land for wine though the high production costs keep the quantity limited. The first vineyards developed in lower Molise around the fifth century BC when the Romans conquered Ancient Samnium. The wine selections include several varieties that are made from classic native grape varieties. Recently, they have also starting using Tintilia which is another ancient native grape variety.

PIEDMONT

Piedmont heartily welcomes the refined ingredients of nearby lands in its local cuisine. In bagna caöda (a magnificent dipping sauce for cooked and raw vegetables) we find the use of salt-packed anchovies, which is a Ligurian specialty that has been traded since ancient times in exchange for the local Piedmont cheeses. In the famous Gnocchi alla Bava specialty, the dominant flavour is Fontina cheese, which comes from Valdosta. Ratatuia (mixed sweet and sour vegetables) is a close relative of the Cote d'Azur's specialty Ratatouille.

The lands of Piedmont also supply a bountiful harvest thanks to the people's dedication, ability, technique and passion with 226 certified traditional products. The local specialties reflect the bounty with square Asti peppers used in a number of different dishes, Barbera and Barolo wine used to cook meats, Langhe truffles used to enhance meats or risottos and hazelnuts used in a variety of desserts. The cuisine is rich and hearty to combat the cold and fog that reign supreme in Piedmont for several months each year.

One last historical anecdote: Marengo-style chicken was invented by Napoleon's chef during the famous battle of 14 June 1800 after requisitioning a few chickens from a local farmer. He cut the chicken into pieces and fried it in olive oil, white wine and parsley. That original rustic dish was then further enriched and perfected by generations of cooks. Some add bay leaves; others add garlic and onion or fried eggs or even mushrooms and crayfish. It is definitely not a light dish but it does truly speak to the palate in beautiful terms.

The desserts are truly amazing with lots of variations on chocolate and hazelnuts. The local quality cocoa bean processing and the Tonda Gentile variety of hazelnuts (with a delicate and unmistakeable flavour) give rise to a plethora of delights including Baci di dama, torroni, nisulin, copeta and gianduia.

WHERE TO FIND PIEDMONTESE SPECIALTIES IN ITALY

CAGLIARI	**L'ARANCERE:** Via Santa Margherita, 19 - Tel.: 070 657433 **RISTORANTE CRACKERS:** Corso Vittorio Emanuele II, 195 - Tel.: 070 653912
FLORENCE	**CAVOLO NERO:** Via dell'Ardiglione, 22 - Tel.: 055 294744
GENOA	**TRATTORIA DA MONSU:** Piazza Nicolò Barabino, 18/R - Tel.: 010 413611
MILAN	**ALLA CUCINA DELLE LANGHE:** Corso Como, 6 - Tel.: 02 6554279 **LA RAVA E LA FAVA:** Via Principe Eugenio, 28 - Tel.: 02 33602175 **TRATTORIA AURORA:** Via Savona, 23 - Tel.: 02 89404978
ROME	**IL TUCANO A TAVOLA:** Via Carlo Mirabello, 10 - Tel.: 06 3728054 **LA PIEMONTESE:** Via Baldo degli Ubaldi, 231 - Tel.: 06 39746536
TURIN	**L'ACINO:** Via San Domenico 2/A - Tel.: 011 5217077 **PARLAPÀ:** Corso Principe Eugenio, 17 - Tel.: 011 4365899 **TAVERNA DELL'OCA:** Via dei Mille, 24 - Tel.: 011 837547

Gnocchi alla bava

750g potatoes (boiled and peeled); 150g buckwheat flour; 200g all purpose flour; 2 eggs;200g of Toma cheese or fresh Fontina cheese; 400g of cream; 1 glass of white wine; 1 white truffle; salt to taste.

This potato dumpling and cream of truffle dish is famous throughout the region and it has been a part of local cuisine for ages. The gnocchi dumplings have always been made with buckwheat flour but through the ages the topping was enriched with a number of French-inspired additions that linked well with the rich locally produced ingredients including cream, cheese and truffle, which make this dish truly unforgettable.

PREPARATION

Rice the potatoes and mix together with the buckwheat and all purpose flour, eggs, a pinch of salt and knead the ingredients well to form smooth, firm dough. Cover the dough and set aside for half an hour. Divide the dough into pieces and roll them with the palm of your hand to make logs around one centimetre in diameter. Cut the logs into three centimetre lengths. Press each piece onto the back of a fork (rolling it gently with your thumb to leave indentions on the dumpling) and then place on a floured tray. Scrub the truffle, rinse it in wine and cut it into very thin slivers. Separately, heat the cream and diced cheese over a very low flame for five minutes while stirring constantly. Cook the gnocchi in a pan of boiling salted water and remove the gnocchi as soon as they float. Place in a warm serving bowl and pour the cream and cheese sauce over the top. Mix well so that the gnocchi dumplings absorb the sauce. Top with truffle slivers and serve.

THE LOCAL PRODUCT

TOMA PIEMONTESE

The origins of Toma Piemontese cheese date back the Imperial Era. However, the first precise written reference with indications dates back to the 11th century. The etymology of the name Toma is unknown; however it is used in Piedmont, Valle d'Aosta, France and Sicily. It may refer to the phase of cheese making when the casein coagulates. In local dialect, this stage is called "tome". In any case, it is still known by its traditional name or Toma from Piedmont where it is produced on the mountains and foothills.

MODERATE

EASY

Panissa

400g rice; 200g dried beans soaked in water for 12 hours;100g of diced fresh lard; ¼ of an onion (chopped); 30g of butter; extra virgin olive oil and salt to taste.

Panissa (or Paniscia) is a bean and rice specialty made from the high quality locally-grown rice. There are a number of versions of the recipe and this one is common in the province of Vercelli. Near Novara they prepare a somewhat heartier version made with Savoy cabbage, tomato, pork rind, salami and red wine.

PREPARATION

Boil the beans in a pan of salted water. Separately brown the diced fresh lard and onion in a little oil. Add the rice and allow it to cook for a few minutes without adding any liquid. When the rice begins to become transparent and golden add the water used to cook the beans one ladleful at a time. Salt to taste and cook for 10 minutes and continue stirring. The dish should be nice and saucy, but not soupy. Add the beans and a little butter, mix and set aside for a couple of minutes before serving.

THE LOCAL PRODUCT

BARBERA D'ALBA

This wine is produced from 100% Barbera d'Alba grapes grown on the hills surrounding Alba in the Cuneo province. This is a popular wine that farmers used in the past to accompany their meals and over the years it has become one of the most popular wines in Italy and the world. It pairs well with the warm local appetizers, first courses with hearty toppings, as well as red meats, chicken and flavourful cheeses.

MODERATE

EASY

Risotto al Barolo

350 g rice; 1 onion; ½ litre meat broth;
½ litre Barolo wine; 1 bay leaf; grated cheese, butter and salt to taste

This creamy risotto is flavourful and has a beautiful colour thanks to the addition of Barolo, Piedmont's most magnificent wine.

PREPARATION

Dice the onion and brown it in butter with the bay leaf. When the onion becomes transparent, add the rice and stir for a minute to lightly toast the rice. Add the wine a little at a time and continue to stir. After the wine has evaporated, add salt and one ladleful of broth. Stir constantly and add broth (one ladleful at a time) until the rice is cooked al dente. Add butter and serve hot with grated cheese.

THE LOCAL PRODUCT

BAROLO WINE This wine is famous for its excellence and in past times it was particularly appreciated by the Count of Cavour and Cesare Pavese. It takes its name from the municipality where it was made – an ancient fief belonging to the Marquis Falletto family which developed the wine (at the beginning of the 19th century). It is made from Nebbiolo grapes cultivated along the hills of eleven towns in Langhe Albesi. Pressed purely, it must be aged at least three years. It pairs well with game, roast meats, flavourful cheeses and truffles.

1 capon; 1 calf head; 300g beef short ribs; 300g beef spare ribs; 200g oxtail; 200g beef tongue; 1 Cotechino sausage; 4 carrots; 4 onions; 4 celery stalks; 4 garlic cloves; rosemary; salt and pepper to taste

Bollito misto

This rich dish of boiled meats was traditionally made from seven prime cuts, seven lesser cuts (including beef, poultry and pork) and it was served with seven dipping sauces. It was ordinarily accompanied by five side dishes (boiled potatoes, spinach and butter, mushrooms, sweet and sour onions and a cup of broth). These days most people use a simplified version with only 5 cuts of meat and 3 dipping sauces: bagnèt vert (a green sauce made from anchovies, parsley, garlic and oil), bagnèt ross (tomato sauce with crushed herbs, garlic, hot red pepper, sugar, vinegar and oil) and saosa'd avijé (or 'sauce of the bees' because it is made from honey mixed with broth, mustard and grated walnuts).

PREPARATION

Fill a large pan with water and a handful of salt, uncut vegetables (1 onion, 1 carrot, and 1 celery stalk), 1 garlic clove, pepper and rosemary. Bring the mixture to a boil and allow it to boil for around 15 minutes before adding the oxtail, spare ribs and short ribs. Cook for another 15 minutes over a high flame then lower the flame and cook for around 2 hours. In another 3 pans boil the tongue, head and capon separately with salt, pepper, ½ an onion, 1 garlic clove, 1 carrot and 1 celery stalk in each pan. The calf head and tongue should cook for two hours but the capon only needs one and a half hours. In another pan of water, cook the cotechino for 1 hour. When the meats are cooked, place them all together in the large pan and cook for a minute to blend the flavours. Drain the meat and prepare it while it is hot. Slice the meat that has already fallen off the bone and debone the rest of the meat (taking care to remove the skin and cartilage) and cut it into pieces. Serve together with the dipping sauces.

THE LOCAL PRODUCT

NEBBIOLO D'ALBA This DOC wine is named for the famous hilly area around Alba, but the famous grape has been cultivated throughout Piedmont for centuries. References from the 13th century speak of the local cultivation of grapes around Rivoli. Nebbiolo grapes are used to make the best known red wines of Piedmont. In past times, this penalized the production of 100% Nebbiolo grape wines. It pairs well with roasts (especially white meats), boiled meats and truffle and cheese specialties. The spumante is an after-dinner specialty.

Brasato al Barolo

800g lean beef roast; 120g flat pancetta cut into strips; 50g butter; 1 bottle of Barolo wine; 2 carrots and 2 celery stalks; 1 onion and 1 garlic clove; 1 twig of rosemary; 3 cloves; 1 bay leaf; flour; thyme; cinnamon, salt and peppercorns to taste.

Beef braised in Barolo wine sauce is a holiday classic. The recipe takes quite a while to prepare but it is truly a delight. When prepared correctly the meat is incredibly tender and bursting with flavour.

PREPARATION

Dice the carrots, celery, onion, garlic. Rinse the herbs and place them in a gauze sack or mesh tea infuser. Make small incisions in the meat with a knife or meat larder and push tiny chunks of pancetta into the incisions (push the pancetta in entirely so that it melts inside the meat when cooking). Place the roast in a large glass bowl and cover the meat with wine. Cover the bowl and allow the meat to marinate in a cool place (not the refrigerator) for around 12 hours taking care to turn the meat every few hours. Brown the remaining pancetta in butter in a large Dutch oven. Drain the meat, dip in flour and brown on each side. Then pour in the marinade and boil. After a few minutes remove the herbs, cover the pan and simmer for at least one hour (turn the meat occasionally). Then remove the meat, allow it to cool and cut it into slices. Use the blender to puree the sauce then add salt and pepper and allow it to simmer until it thickens. Pour the sauce on the meat and serve.

THE LOCAL PRODUCT

BARBARESCO WINE This incredible wine is made from grapes that are cultivated in the heart of the Langhe area. It is named for Barbaresco, a town located on the hills of Alba in an area crossed by the Tanaro River, where the wine is made. This ancient wine was even cited by Titus Livius in his History of Rome. It was later rediscovered and popularized at the end of the 1800s by Domizio Cavazza, the Director of the School of Oenological Studies in Alba. This aged wine has an intense flavour that accompanies roasts, braised meats, game, poultry and flavourful cheese magnificently.

TIME CONSUMING

AVERAGE

TIME CONSUMING

EASY

Bagna Cauda

300g of cleaned cardoons (remove all leaves, pare the entire length of the stalk to remove the strings on the outside of the stalk and the thin silver sheath on the inside of the stalk); 2 cleaned peppers (remove seeds and pith and cut into fillets); 2 carrots cut into thin slices; 200g of Savoy cabbage (use the centre heart leaves); 100g of cleaned radicchio; 2 cleaned leaks cut into half; 4 slices of fried winter squash; 4 boiled potatoes; 4 onions (cleaned and baked); 300g of steamed cauliflower; 8 salted anchovy fillets; 8 garlic cloves (peeled); 40g butter; extra virgin olive oil and salt to taste

Cuisine in Piedmont falls into two major categories: it is composed of delicate flavours like cream and cheese or robust flavours with lots of anchovies. This traditionally famous dipping sauce is a little like fondue and it definitely falls in with the robust flavours. This specialty is used as a side dish, but it is also substantial enough to skip the first course – especially if you serve the dipping sauce accompanied by a few slices of toasted polenta. The vegetables mentioned are only suggestions; you can make substitutions as you please according to your preference and the season.

PREPARATION

Remove the green sprout from the garlic centre and slice the garlic into slivers. Place the garlic and anchovies in a ceramic pan, top with oil and cook covered over a very low flame for half an hour. The ingredients should fall apart without browning. Add the butter and serve in a fondue pot to keep the sauce warm. Serve the dipping sauce with the vegetables listed in the ingredients.

THE LOCAL PRODUCT

ALBUGNANO DOC WINE

The grapes are cultivated in upper Asti in the valleys of the "Lower Monferrato" hill country. The main grape used in Albugnano is the Nebbiolo grape which gives the wines truly distinct and identifiable characteristics. The red is a perfect dinner wine that pairs well with first courses with meat sauces or mushrooms, stewed meats, roasts and boiled meats as well as flavourful cheeses. The rosé is magnificent with the local specialty Bagna Cauda.

Baci di dama

150g flour; 1 egg yolk;
100g dark chocolate;
150g almonds (or hazelnuts) shelled and blanched;
100g sugar;
100g butter

PREPARATION

Mix the sugar and almonds in the blender. Then mix the flour, eggs and butter (the butter needs to be at room temperature) and mix well. Butter and flour a baking pan and roll out small balls of dough and place the balls (they should not touch one another) on the baking pan. Bake at 180° Celsius for around ten minutes. Remove from the oven and let the cookies cool completely. In the meantime, melt the chocolate in a double boiler. Dip the flat side of two cookies into the chocolate and then press the two cookies together to form a chocolate seal. Repeat the procedure for all the cookies, cool and serve.

MODERATE

EASY

These refined chocolate and nut cookies were invented over a century ago in the town of Tortona, but they have been a specialty throughout all Italian patisserie shops for quite some time. Aside from the classic recipe, there are also great variations with hazelnuts used in place of the almonds or the addition of candied orange grated into the dough.

THE LOCAL PRODUCT

HAZELNUTS FROM PIEDMONT Hazelnuts originated in Asia Minor and made their way to Italy thanks to the Greeks. In Piedmont, hazelnuts were grown together with other crops for personal consumption or local confectionary purposes until the middle of the eighteen hundreds. Between the 1800s and 1900s demand grew considerably as did the production of hazelnuts for chocolate specialties and gianduia (chocolate mixed with hazelnut paste). Gianduia is used by the confectionary industry to prepare traditional dessert specialties from Piedmont (including Gianduia chocolates, Torrone d'Alba nougat, cream pralines and caramel nougat.

TIME CONSUMING

DIFFICULT

Bônet

1 litre milk; 5 eggs; 50g bitter cocoa; 200g sugar;
3 tablespoons of very strong espresso; 2 teaspoons of rum;
2 teaspoons Marsala wine; 100g ladyfingers; 100g amaretto cookies

Bônet is an amazing creamy dessert that is a traditional specialty throughout Piedmont. There are a number of different local variations: some recipes use amaretto cookies without any ladyfingers while others call for vanilla or lemon zest to flavour the dessert instead of coffee and liqueur - all the versions make a truly delicate and enjoyable dessert.

PREPARATION

Boil the milk and allow it to cool. Break the cookies into the milk and add the coffee and liqueur. In a separate dish mix the eggs with the sugar and cocoa and blend until it forms a smooth cream. Add the milk and cookies to the cream while mixing constantly. Caramelise the pudding mould: place part of the sugar in the mould and hold the mould over the flame until the sugar begins to caramelise (rotate the mould well so that the caramel covers the bottom and sides completely). Fill the mould with the prepared mixture and cook it in a double boiler in the oven at 200° Celsius for around 40 minutes. Remove from the oven, cool and refrigerate for a couple of hours. Turn the pudding out onto a dish and serve.

THE LOCAL PRODUCT

BRACHETTO D'ACQUI
The production area includes 26 municipalities in the Asti and Alessandria provinces. The heart of the production lands for this DOCG wine is near Aqui, an area with thermal springs at the edge of Monferrato. The grapes are most likely native to the Asti-Monferrini hills. Two varieties are available including the aromatic Brachetto del Piemonte and Brachetto di Nizza Marittima. The young wine is also available in a bubbly version. Sweet and aromatic, it exalts the flavour of strawberries and peaches and pairs magnificently with fruit salads and sorbets. It also accompanies traditional desserts and cookies.

PUGLIA

From the plains known as the 'Table of Apulius' to the Murgia plateaus continuing on to the Umbra Forest and the rocky coast of Gargano... we find a plethora of flavours and expressions of nature all closely linked to a historically important local ingredient: hard grain wheat (which may be the best in Italy). This gave rise to a long tradition of pasta recipes including both high quality drawn pasta, as well as eggless handmade pasta. We find the most famous local pasta specialty called orecchiette, as well as a number of other great recipes. Hard grain wheat is also used to make great local bread that is long-lasting and stays fresh for many days like Altamura bread. Toasted dried bread or "freselle" are soaked and topped with tasty ingredients for quick snacks. Hard grain wheat also gives rise to another tasty famous specialty called "tarallo" which are round crackers with a texture similar to pretzels that are also a specialty in the nearby Campania and Basilicata regions

A host of delights are created with the fine local produce and an endless array of fragrant recipes are topped with the local olive oil, which has gained popularity in recent years. The sheep and cow milk cheeses are both excellent with a wide variety of dairy specialties including pecorino, mozzarella, nodini, mozzarella braids, incredible giuncata and ricotta forte which is eaten plain or used to enhance a number of recipes.

There are also a number of meat specialties such as Gnummarieddi lamb rolls that can be tasted in the Middle of July at the Sagra della Carne Ferrata festival. There are also a number of pork specialties including prosciutto from Faeto, a type of wild black boar, soppressata salami with vino cotto, or sanguinaccio di Lecce with a slight orange zest aroma.

The long coastline makes for a rich list of seafood specialties. Visiting Puglia in the spring is truly enchanting with all the almond trees in bloom. The almonds inspired local dessert specialties with marzipan, almond milk and a wide range of cakes and cookies that are frequently sweetened with the fine local honey.

WHERE TO FIND APULIAN SPECIALTIES IN ITALY

BARI	**AL PESCATORE:** Piazza Federico II di Svevia, 6 - Tel.: 080 5237039
	LA BRUSCHETTA: Via Sagarriga Visconti, 13 - Tel.: 080 5214382
	OSTERIA DEI QUATTRO GATTI: Via Cardinal A. Ciasca, 17 - Tel.: 080 5043446
BOLOGNA	**IL CANTUCCIO:** Via Volturno, 4 - Tel.: 051 233424
	OFFICINE DEGLI APULI: Via S.Lorenzo, 4 - Tel.: 051 236042
	OSTERIA DEL CIRMOLO: Via San Felice 86/A - Tel.: 051 522432
BOLZANO	**AMADÈ:** Vicolo Cà de' Bezzi, 8 - Tel.: 0471 300105
MILAN	**IL RIFUGIO PUGLIESE:** Via Costanza, 2 - Tel.: 02 48000917
	OSTERIA RAP DEL GARGANO: Via Andrea Verga, 16 - Tel.: 02 462715
	RISTORANTE ALBEROBELLO: Via Andrea Solari, 60 - Tel.: 02 474827
PALERMO	**4 PASSI:** Via Giovanni da Cartagena, 14 - Tel.: 091 6893040
ROME	**CIME DI RAPE:** Corso di Francia, 207 - Tel.: 06 36303752
	I TRULLI CANTERINI: Via Trionfale, 9516 - Tel.: 06 3385510
	LA CAPAGIRA: Via Voghera, 10 - Tel.: 06 7012811
TURIN	**PIZZERIA LA GARGANICA:** Via Carlo Alberto, 18 - Tel.: 011 538889
	RISTORANTE LA CAMPANA: Via XX Settembre, 79/E - Tel.: 011 5214011
	VECCHIA CANOSA: Piazza Ottorino Respighi, 9 - Tel.: 011 284700
TRIESTE	**LE 10 REGINE:** Via Milano, 14 - Tel.: 040 3478754
VENICE	**AVOGARIA:** Calle Dell'Avogaria, 1629 - Tel.: 041 2960491

Calzone

TIME CONSUMING

EASY

250g flour; 10g brewer's yeast;
200g juicy tomatoes (peeled and cut into chunks);
80g ricotta salata cheese (dry salted ricotta);
50g pitted black olives; onion, extra virgin olive oil and salt to taste

This is a truly tasty pizza pie.
A diced anchovy version is a popular Lenten specialty.

PREPARATION

Dilute the brewer's yeast with a little water. Mix the flour, salt and half a cup of oil. Knead the dough until it has an elastic texture then cover it and set it aside to rise for one hour. In the meantime brown the thinly sliced onion in a little oil. Add the olives and tomatoes cut into pieces, salt and pepper and cook for another 5 to 10 minutes then take it off the stove and mix in the ricotta salata. Roll out two sheets of dough and use the larger one to line an oiled baking pan (taking care that the dough covers the sides of the pan). Lay a layer of the filling over the top and then cover it with the smaller crust. Use a fork to punch holes in the crust before baking at 240° Celsius for 20 minutes.

THE LOCAL PRODUCT

BELLA DELLA DAUNIA OLIVES

Bella della Daunia olives are cultivated on a large sunny plain. The fertility of the land and the temperate climate in the area gave rise to a number of different settlements (Italian, Spanish, French and Belgian) which each introduced various species of plants including Spanish olives known as “Bella di Cerignola” named for the town where they were most popular. Some authors believe that this variety of olive derives from the Roman “Orchites and others believe it derived from Spanish olives imported before the 1400s. Either way Bella della Daunia may be considered as a new native variety with better qualities than the original one both as far as quality is concerned (pit to pulp ratio) and as far as organoleptic qualities are concerned due to the sun and type of soil.

Orecchiette alle cime di rapa

400g orecchiette pasta (fresh or packaged); 400g turnip greens;
1 red pepper; 2 garlic cloves;
extra virgin olive oil and salt to taste

MODERATE

EASY

This is Puglia's most popular pasta dish. These small round ear-shaped pasta shells (orecchiette means 'little ears') are great served a number of ways because they hold the sauce well. This is the original and most traditional recipe.

PREPARATION

Clean and chop the turnip greens. Parboil the greens in a very large pan filled with salted water (set aside the water used to boil the greens after draining and squeezing them). Brown the diced garlic and hot pepper. Then add the turnip greens and salt and cook over a high flame for a couple of minutes. In the meantime cook the pasta in the water used to boil the greens. Cook the pasta until it is al dente, drain and mix it together with the greens over a high flame.

THE LOCAL PRODUCT

PRIMITIVO DI MANDURIA WINE

The name of this grape (Primitivo) refers to the fact that the variety is harvested early. Native to the Ionian-Salento coasts, the grape variety is grown throughout the Murge area in the town of Manduria and the lands around it. The table wine is perfect for flavourful salami, rich first courses with meat, roasts, game and flavourful cheeses. The dolce naturale is perfect with unleavened desserts, almond-stuffed figs, fruit pies, mostaccioli cookies, fried cheeses with honey and spices, cakes and amaretto. The liquoroso naturale is a complex wine that commands reflection: it is perfect with rich creamy liqueur cakes. The liquoroso secco is best with baked desserts and tozzetti cookies.

Pancotto con rucola

400g of dry hard-grain bread; 400g rucola (wild is best);
2 medium potatoes; 1 zucchini; 150g green beans;
2 juicy ripe tomatoes; 50g pancetta; 1 onion;
extra virgin olive oil, red pepper and salt to taste

This soup is a great way to use dry bread and wild greens (like rucola) mixed with garden fresh vegetables. This simple rural dish is worthy of note.

PREPARATION

Wash, peel and cut the vegetables and rucola into pieces. Simmer in a large pot of salted water for one hour. In the meantime brown the onion and pancetta in a little oil and hot pepper and add it to the soup. When the soup is a two-thirds of the way cooked, drop in slices of dry bread, mix and continue cooking for 15 minutes. Top with a little olive oil, stir and set aside for 10 minutes before serving.

THE LOCAL PRODUCT

INITIALLED BREAD

With agricultural roots, the inhabitants of the upper Murgia area still make bread the same way – sourdough, natural leavening, sea salt and water in a wood burning oven. The most traditional shape of bread known as 'U sckuanète' or stacked bread was very large in size. It was generally kneaded at home and cooked in the public ovens. The baker would stamp each loaf with a wooden or metal brand with the family initials. The essential characteristic of this bread was that it was long lasting because the farmers and shepherds needed a food source that could last a week or even fifteen days during the time they spent on the large farms in the high murgia plains. The food source of these people (almost exclusively) was bread dipped in boiling water and topped with oil and salt.

MODERATE

EASY

Simuledda

4 tablespoons of polenta flour; 2 litres vegetable or meat broth; 200g sliced potatoes; 350g of wild fennel (cleaned and cut into pieces); 100g grated cheese; extra virgin olive oil and salt to taste

The traditional philosophy behind this fragrant soup from Foggia is simple: use what you can gather. In this case the incredibly fragrant wild fennel plants are the key to this unusual and refined dish.

PREPARATION

Boil the wild fennel and potatoes in broth. After the broth begins to boil, start adding the polenta flour slowly while mixing. Add salt and cook for 20 minutes and then serve with a topping of grated cheese and a dash of olive oil.

THE LOCAL PRODUCT

SAN SEVERO DOC WINE

The grapes are cultivated on the hills between Foggia and the Molise border on the southern end of the long plain near the Gargano promontory in a town named San Severo that is surrounded by grape vineyards in a large zone known as Capitanata di Puglia. They have been cultivating grapes here since the Imperial Era. The white wine is a delight with seafood dishes and fresh cheeses. The rosé and the red are best with first courses with meat sauces, pork or beef specialties, spicy salami and flavourful cheeses.

Tiella di riso e cozze

200g rice; 800g cleaned mussels; 400g sliced potatoes; diced fresh lard, diced onion, diced garlic and diced red pepper; oil, salt and pepper to taste

TIME CONSUMING | EASY

A 'tiella' is a characteristic local layered dish that makes a hearty first course. This rice and mussel tiella is a perfect way to start an important lunch.

PREPARATION

Cook the mussels in a large pan with a little oil and a dash of pepper until they open. As soon as the mussel shells open, drain the mussels and allow them to cool before shelling them. Set aside the water from the mussels. Brown the diced mixture in a Dutch oven with oil. Then add 1½ litres of salted water and the potatoes. Boil for ten minutes and then add the rice and cook over a high flame. When the rice has almost finished cooking add the mussels (and the liquid set aside from cooking them). Check for salt and cook for a couple of minutes (mixing well) before serving.

THE LOCAL PRODUCT

SALICE SALENTINO WINE

This DOC certified wine is from the Ionian-Salento region where they have grown grapes since antiquity in the provinces of Brindisi and Lecce. The heart of the production area is Salice Salentino and the surrounding areas. The white pairs well with pasta and rice dishes, seafood and vegetables. The red is best with stuffed pasta shells, red meats, game and flavourful cheeses; The rosé accompanies spicy salami, light first courses, white and red meats, vegetables, egg dishes and fresh cheeses. The dolce versions make a perfect pairing for desserts and traditional sweets.

MODERATE

EASY

Triglia alle erbe

4 red mullet weighing 200g each, cleaned; 2 garlic cloves; 4 tablespoons of breadcrumbs; a mixture of aromatic herbs including parsley, basil, rosemary, sage and marjoram; flour, extra virgin olive oil, salt and pepper to taste

Mullet enveloped by a cloud of fragrant herbs. This dish has an incredible aroma that explodes in flavour at the first bite - a simple and thoroughly enjoyable recipe.

PREPARATION

Rinse and dry the mullet. Make small cuts on both sides of the fish and dip the mullet in flour. Prepare a diced mixture of garlic, parsley, basil, part of the breadcrumbs, oil, salt and pepper. Use this mixture to line the bottom of a baking pan. Place the mullet on top of the herbs and make a second diced herb mixture of rosemary, sage, marjoram and the rest of the breadcrumbs, oil and salt. Cover the fish with the second mixture and bake at 200° Celsius until the crust is golden brown.

THE LOCAL PRODUCT

OLIVES FROM PUGLIA

Puglia has been the land of olives par excellence since ancient times with a patrimony of over 44 million olive trees in the region. Olive cultivation is a mainstay of the landscape and local economy and it is good for the environment and the landscape. Olives have been cultivated in the Foggia province since the Imperial Era and Daunia is the ancient name of the Foggia province. In later times, the oil industry developed further thanks to sea trade.

Lampascioni in agro

MODERATE

EASY

500g muscari comosum bulbs (wild grape hyacinth bulbs); mint leaves, white wine vinegar; extra virgin olive oil, salt and pepper to taste

Lampascioni are edible muscari (wild grape hyacinth) bulbs that look like tiny onions. These characteristic bulbs have a unique and pleasant flavour that is even further exalted by this recipe.

PREPARATION

After having cleaned the muscari bulbs and removing the leaves, place them in water and soak for at least 24 hours (change the water periodically). This procedure helps to eliminate any excess bitterness. Boil the bulbs in a large pan of salted water and cook until they can be pierced easily with a fork. Drain and place the bulbs on a serving dish. Top with vinegar, salt, coarse ground pepper and mint leaves. Serve after 1 hour.

THE LOCAL PRODUCT

EDIBLE MUSCARI

The Lampascione or edible muscari bulb is the flavour of Puglia. This wild grape hyacinth blooms in spring and it grows from a small onion-like bulb that is present throughout the interior lands. With a million different names, it is not actually a hyacinth, but a member of the lily family with a bright blue flower. Another food that could be gathered locally, it was a favourite among poorer families and it has been eaten longer than anyone can remember - back when gathering food was the most common method for procuring it. Traditionally, this dish is eaten during Lent, which is in accordance with the production period of the plant. The bulb is very bitter, but the way it is prepared reduces the bitterness until it is just a pleasant hint. In Acaya di Vernole in the Lecce province, they hold a Lampascione festival (Te li pampasciuni) in honour of Our Lady of Sorrows.

MODERATE

EASY

Dita degli apostoli

These ricotta-stuffed crepe rolls are a variation on a common Italian specialty known as ricotta farcita. The filling can be made in a number of different ways (coffee, pie cherries or sweet cherries in liqueur).

8 small crêpes made with orange zest;
300g sheep-milk ricotta;
80g sugar;
the juice of 1 lemon;
orange syrup to taste

PREPARATION

Place the ricotta in a strainer for around 1 hour to drain before mixing the ingredients together. Mix well to form a creamy filling. Put a spoonful of filling at the centre of each crepe then roll it and cut it into three pieces. Lay the pieces on a plate and cover with orange syrup (cook sugar and orange juice together to form the syrup).

THE LOCAL PRODUCT

CITRUS FROM GARGANO
The most ancient reference to the prestige of the citrus fruits grown in the Gargano area dates back to the year 1000. Prince Melo gave some to the Normans to help convince them to conquer Puglia. At the end of the seventeen hundreds Wolfgang Goethe was attracted by the incredible biodiversity in the area later and later wrote of it in his famous diary "Italian Journey". The era of greatest wealth in Gargano was during the second half of the eighteen hundreds thanks to the flowering citrus export industry.

SARDINIA

The isolation of this splendid island gave rise to the incredible diversity of Sardinia and its unmistakeable character with a different language, sounds and forms. The myriad of delicious flavours are the result of this diversity.

The local traditions are divided into two main groups: the inland peoples (shepherds and farmers) and the seafaring peoples who lived along the 1500 km coastline. The characteristic meat preparations such as "su carraxiu" come from the shepherds. The dish calls for pieces of meat wrapped in reeds and buried in the ground. The hole is recovered and a fire is built on top while the meat cooks slowly beneath it slowly enhancing the flavours. The Sardinian landscape offers a number of aromatic herbs including: bay leaves, juniper and myrtle (used to make Sardinia's famous mirto liqueur). The lands are used to free range magnificent Modicana beef cows (which is a rare breed). The lamb and kid are also excellent and the area also offers excellent wild boar and salami including wine sausages, capocollo and the very unique mustela (the name actually means weasel due to the long thin shape of this salami made from local pork sirloin) which is aromatized and seasoned. The pastoral lifestyle also gave rise to a number of cheese specialties including the famous Casizolu from Santu Lussurgiu – a pear-shaped cacio cheese made from Modicane breed milk cows or from Merka, a sour cream cheese made from goat or sheep milk and the famous Fiore Sardo, a very popular sheep milk cheese.

The fish dishes are also amazingly simple. The fish is frequently roasted plain without anything in order to preserve its flavour. The sea offers long lasting specialties as well as a great fresh catch. In Sardinia we find Musciamme (salted tuna) or botargo (salted tuna or grey mullet roe). The many kinds of breads and desserts are magnificent with the frequent addition of almonds, raisins, myrtle and Sardinia's fantastic apples, especially the Asfodelo and Sulla varieties. The Italian Corbezzolo (Arbutus Unedo or Strawberry Tree) is another local fruit that pairs perfectly with the flavourful cheeses.

WHERE TO FIND SARDINIAN SPECIALTIES IN ITALY

BOLOGNA	**HOSTARIA SAN CARLINO:** Via San Carlo, 16 - Tel.: 051 267496 **OSTERIA DEL MONTESINO:** Via del Pratello, 74 - Tel.: 051 523426
BOLZANO	**IL NURAGHE:** Via Claudia Augusta, 67 - Tel.: 0471 266536 **SA DOMOMEA:** Doktor Streiter Gasse, 7 - Tel.: 0471 972641
CAGLIARI	**CI PENSA CANNAS:** Via Sardegna, 37 - Tel.: 070 667815 **SA DOMU SARDA:** Via Sassari, 51 - Tel.: 070 653400 **SA TURRA:** Corso Vittorio Emanuele, 126 - Tel.: 070 663191
FLORENCE	**LA BIRITULLERA:** Via Pietro Cironi, 4 - Tel.: 055 496225
GENOA	**RISTORANTE PINTORI:** Via San Bernardo, 68/R - Tel.: 010 2757507 **TRATTORIA THARROS:** Via Germano Jori, 124 - Tel.: 010 6443071
MILAN	**BAIA CHIA:** Via Antonio Bazzini, 37 - Tel.: 02 2361131 **IL VELIERO 23:** Via Decembrio, 26 - Tel.: 02 5460663
ROME	**HOSTARIA MAMUTONES:** Piazza Monte Gennaro, 29 - Tel.: 06 8185237 **IL GARIGLIANO:** Via Garigliano, 70/A - Tel.: 06 8551077
TURIN	**ANDROMEDA:** Via Francesco Petrarca, 8 - Tel.: 011 6505641 **RISTORANTE SARDEGNA:** Via San Donato, 27 - Tel.: 011 484832
VENICE	**RISTORANTE L'INCONTRO:** Dorsoduro, 3062 - Tel.: 041 2771125

Pane frattau

QUICK

EASY

4 rounds of pane carasau (cracker-like flatbread); 4 eggs; 100g Pecorino Sardo cheese slivers; 1 cup of simple sauce made from tomato sauce, oil and salt;
1 cup of white wine vinegar; salt to taste.

This egg and bread specialty was a common dish amongst shepherds during their long trips away from home. Initially the dish only called for flatbread, broth and grated cheese (frattau means grated in Sardinian). With time the dish was enriched with other ingredients and this version makes a hearty opening dish or a tasty snack.

PREPARATION

Wet each piece of flatbread with very hot salted water and lay one on each plate. Top with tomato sauce and cheese. Boil the water and vinegar and break the eggs into the mixture (one at a time) after it begins to boil. Remove the eggs with a skimmer after three minutes and place one on the centre of each round disk of flatbread.

THE LOCAL PRODUCT

SARDINIAN BREAD
Bread is an absolutely important staple in Sardinian cuisine. The poverty of the region, the constant risk of famine and long voyages far from home (especially for the shepherds) inspired Sardinian cooks to invent bread that was very long lasting and easy to transport. This fascination with bread gave rise to a number of tasty recipes such as pane frattau (an egg and bread specialty), zuppa gallurese (bread and cabbage soup), pane guttiau (bread with melted cheese and oil). One of the most popular types of breads is named Pane Carasau, which is a flatbread that is also known as 'sheet music' bread in Italian because it is so large and so flat. There are few ingredients in Pane Carasau: flour, water, yeast and salt – the trick is all in the preparation. After raising for about 4 hours the dough is rolled out to create 2 millimetre thick round crusts. The crusts are baked individually in the oven and when the dough puffs up; it is removed from the oven and divided into two sheets with a knife. Each sheet is then baked in the oven again for a couple of minutes to brown.

TIME CONSUMING

DIFFICULT

Culurgiones

400g of all purpose flour and durum semolina flour mixed together; 15g rendered lard; 500g fresh grated sheep milk cheese; 3 eggs; 350g parboiled Swiss chard; 100g of grated Fiore Sardo cheese; 400g of Bolognese sauce; 1g saffron; salt and pepper to taste.

It seems that stuffed pasta shells made their way into Sardinian cuisine through contact with the Genoese. The Sardinians however took them to a whole new level. This traditional holiday dish of stuffed pasta shells can be made in a number of different shapes with many different toppings. It makes a tasty and festive dish.

PREPARATION

Squeeze any excess liquid from the Swiss chard and dice. Place the greens in a mixing bowl and add grated pecorino cheese and the saffron dissolved in a few drops of warm water, the egg, a tablespoon of flour and knead together for 15 minutes. Prepare the pasta dough separately. Cut the lard into the flour then add a little warm water and salt. Knead for 15 minutes then cover and set aside for a half an hour before rolling out a thin sheet of dough. Place walnut size spoonfuls of the filling onto one half of the dough (5 centimetres apart). Fold the other half of the dough over the top and use a pasta knife to cut out the pasta (taking care to seal the edges). They are frequently folded into a square or crescent shape depending on local preferences. Place the culurgiones on a floured surface, cover and set aside for 12 hours. Boil briefly in a large pan of salted water, drain and top with grated Fiore Sardo cheese and the Bolognese sauce.

THE LOCAL PRODUCT

SARDINIAN SAFFRON

Saffron comes from the Crocus Sativus, a tiny plant that is cultivated on 19 hectares in Sardinia primarily in the San Gavino municipality (all the rest of Italy only accounts for 24-25 hectares of saffron cultivations). The farmers call it Red Sardinian Saffron due to the colour of the threads, but it may be closer to Sardinian gold if we consider the profitability of the variety cultivated here. Due to the high concentration of saffron in San Gavino Monreale, it should be considered as Italy's saffron capital.

Malloreddus

300g flour; 250g fresh Pecorino Sardo cheese;
1 saffron sachet; salt to taste.

Malloreddus are a ridged short pasta shell that is a traditional Sardinian specialty. They can be prepared with a number of different toppings. This extremely simple recipe has only three ingredients (pasta, pecorino sardo cheese and saffron) and it is a sure hit.

PREPARATION

Sift the flour on a dough board, add a pinch of salt and mix with warm water and knead to form firm smooth dough. Wrap the pasta dough in plastic wrap and set aside for half an hour. Roll the dough into 1/2 centimetre cylinders and cut into 1½ centimetre lengths. Press each length of pasta onto the back of a fork with your thumb to create ridges on one side. Allow the pasta to dry on a floured surface and then cook in a large pot of salted water. In the meantime melt the cheese in a double boiler (mix with a wooden spoon). Add the saffron dissolved in half a cup of water from the pasta and mix carefully. Drain the pasta and add it to the melted cheese mixture. Serve steaming hot.

THE LOCAL PRODUCT

PECORINO SARDO CHEESE
They have been making sheep milk cheese on the island of Sardinia as long as they have been shepherding. The first documented references date back to the end of the 1700s. At that time cheeses were made with unpasteurized milk or milk that was heated by dunking boiling rocks in it and the cheeses were divided into three categories known as whites, fine reds and smoked. The fine red and smoked versions are considered to be the progenitors of Pecorino Sardo Cheese. Another typical sheepherder's cheese known in Sardinia as Semicotto was also included under the Pecorino Sardo trademark. At the end of the 1800s, cheese production became industrialized (up to that time it was only produced for local consumption). Today both varieties of Pecorino Sardo cheese (dolce=mild and mature=sharp) are a couple of Italy's most famous cheeses throughout the world.

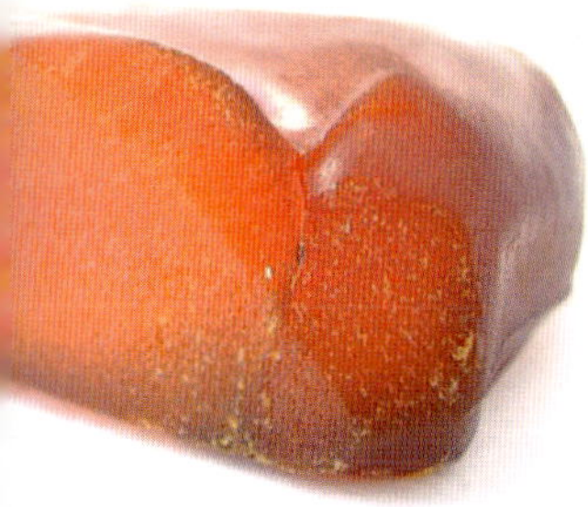

Spaghetti con la bottarga

400g spaghetti (or linguine);
100g botargo (tuna or mullet roe); 2 garlic cloves;
red pepper; extra virgin olive oil and salt to taste

Botargo is what gives this dish pizzazz. In this very simple spaghetti and botargo recipe this exquisite seafood preparation triumphs.

QUICK

EASY

PREPARATION

Brown the garlic and hot pepper in oil for a few minutes. Remove the skin from the outside of the botargo and then grate. In the meantime cook the spaghetti al dente in a large pan of salted water. Drain the spaghetti and pour into the pan with oil and mix well over a high flame for a couple of minutes. Top with botargo, mix and serve.

THE LOCAL PRODUCT

BOTARGO MULLET ROE
The ovaries of the mullet are carefully removed without cutting them and then they are salted with sea salt or brine. After that they are set aside to absorb the salt and then they are rinsed and placed on a slanted counter and pressed to remove any excess liquid. Finally they are allowed to air dry or they are dried under salt for a few days. The botargo is ready when it is firm, compact and the external membrane is well attached to the eggs, which are a uniform tawny colour without any black spots or colour variations. The botargo is stored in a dry ventilated area and used as a condiment or appetizer with artichokes and olive oil.

Burrida

TIME CONSUMING

AVERAGE

700g spotted dogfish (cleaned and skinned); 1 carrot,
1 onion and 1 celery stalk; 4 lemon wedges;
3 tablespoons crushed walnuts and pine nuts; 2 garlic cloves;
1 glass of white wine; extra virgin olive oil and salt

This magnificent sweet and sour seafood salad makes a perfect choice for summer dining.

PREPARATION

Clean the fish, remove the heads and cut into pieces. Place the fish in a pan with hot water then add salt, diced onion, celery and carrot and lemon. Cook for around 10 minutes, remove the fish and place on a serving dish. In another pan brown the crushed garlic and ground nuts, then add vinegar and cook for 5 minutes. Pour the sauce over the fish and marinate for at least 12 hours.

THE LOCAL PRODUCT

EXTRA VIRGIN OLIVE OIL FROM SARDINIA
In Sardinia, olive oil is made from selected olives harvested from October to November in northern Sardinia (Sennori, Sorso, Sassari, Alghero and Ittiri). It has an intense fruity fragrance with a slightly spicy and pleasantly pungent taste.

Capretto al mirto

800g kid goat cut into large pieces; 100g fresh lard cut into thin slices; 50g of the following diced herbs: basil, parsley and myrtle; 1 garlic clove, bread crumbs, extra virgin olive oil, salt and pepper to taste

Kid and lamb are common Sardinian specialties thanks to the excellent quality of the meat. This recipe for kid and myrtle berries is even better thanks to the fresh lard and myrtle that flavour the meat.

PREPARATION

Salt the meat and wrap each piece in a slice of non-rendered lard. Bake at 180° Celsius for half an hour in an oiled pan basting occasionally with the drippings. Dice the herbs and garlic and mix with a few tablespoons of breadcrumbs and oil. Sprinkle the mixture onto the kid after it has cooked for half an hour. Place the pan back in the oven and bake until it forms a golden crust.

THE LOCAL PRODUCT

SARDINIAN MIRTO
This exquisite liqueur made from myrtle berries has a sweet flavour and a natural amber colour. It is made from an ancient Sardinian traditional recipe. It is basically an infusion of myrtle berries in pure alcohol. Mirto from Sardinia contains the aroma and wholesomeness of the Mediterranean plant. Myrtle is a wild evergreen bush that is diffused throughout the Mediterranean and particularly in Sardinia. It grows in temperate climates in any kind of soil. The plant is easy to recognise with shiny leaves and white fragrant flowers with round bluish seeds. The liqueur is great as a digestive and its pleasantly aromatic qualities are best appreciated over ice.

Orata picchettata

1 Gilthead Sea bream (800g cleaned); 4 anchovy fillets cut into half; 8 strips of fresh lard (no longer than 2cm long); 1 glass dry white wine; extra virgin olive oil, salt and pepper to taste.

TIME CONSUMING

AVERAGE

Differently than what you might expect fresh lard and fish make a perfect pairing in this surprisingly delicate seafood specialty which is perfectly enhanced with anchovies.

PREPARATION

Make incisions in the surface of the meat with a knife or larder and stick pieces of anchovy and lard inside the holes. Top the fish with oil, salt and pepper and bake in an oiled pan at 180° Celsius for around 40 minutes. Remove the pan and place on a serving dish. Pour a glass of wine into the pan with the drippings and cook until half the liquid evaporates. Then pour the hot thickened sauce over the top of the fish and serve.

THE LOCAL PRODUCT

VERMENTINO DI SARDEGNA WINE

This wine is made from Vermentino grapes that are grown throughout the region. The grapes originated in Spain and are grown all along the coast of the Mediterranean. The variety reached Sardinia in fairly recent times during the last century and began in the north to then spread throughout the south. The area turned out to be a perfect habitat for the grapes and over time cultivation intensified giving rise to high quality wines. Perfect as an appetizer, it is great with lobster, seafood, fish chowder, botargo, grilled oily fish and smoked salmon. The spumante version is a perfect pair for fruit pies and cookies.

Seadas

250g flour; 200g Fiore Sardo cheese (grated); 1 lemon; 1 orange; 1 shot of grappa; 200g chestnut honey; rendered lard, extra virgin olive oil and powdered sugar to taste.

THE LOCAL PRODUCT

FIORE SARDO CHEESE
Fiore Sardo cheese was invented long ago even before the Roman conquest. At the end of the 1700s Father Francesco Gemelli wrote about the commercial production of pecorino Fiore Sardo cheese. In the 1800s, Fiore sardo was the only cheese exported from Sardinia and it was especially loved by merchants in Naples, Livorno and Genoa (in fact the Genoese used it to prepare their traditional specialty, pesto sauce. The name Fiore Sardo means Sardinian Flower and it most likely derives from the historical production method when it was made in wooden forms with a flower embossed, which left a flower design on the cheese.

This is a very popular and unusual specialty with a delicate citrus fragrance - fried pastries filled with savoury Fiore Sardo cheese and topped with sweet honey.

PREPARATION

Grate the citrus zest and place in a bowl. Add the grated cheese and grappa and mix well. In a separate bowl cut the lard into the flour and then add warm water and mix. Knead the dough well and then roll out a thin pastry sheet. Cut out rounds of dough (12cm diameter) and place a large spoonful of the filling on half of the dough piece. Fold the other half over the top and press down well to seal the edges. Deep fry until golden brown and place on paper towels to absorb any excess oil. Place the Seadas on a serving dish and top with heated honey and a sprinkle of powdered sugar.

SICILY

All cuisine reflects the influences of different culinary traditions and in Sicily it is a true tribute to multiculturalism. Having been ruled by a number of different powers, this land has a complex history. The Phoenicians, Greeks, Romans, Arabs, Normans, French and Spanish all controlled Sicily at one time and each culture influenced the local traditions. The Arab influence can be seen in the unusual pairing of sweet and savoury flavours as well as the introduction of eggplant, a number of spices, rice and almonds: products that have a predominant role in many traditional Sicilian recipes. In Trapani, couscous, which is also eaten in many North African countries, is a common specialty made from semolina. Couscous provides a culinary bond between the peoples of the Mediterranean and there is even an international couscous festival that is constantly growing in popularity. Stockfish was introduced by the Normans while the Spanish specialties, which were already influenced by Arabian traditions, added strong and contrasting flavour combinations (such as olives and oranges, or anchovy paste with delicate pine nuts and raisins). Capers are a truly unmistakeable Sicilian signature specialty – they are native to this sunny rock-strewn land that is crisscrossed by rock walls where these plants find a perfect habitat.

Another unique local product is the Pachino tomato (and real Pachino tomatoes only grow in Sicily). It is used in a wide range of recipes together with bell peppers and eggplant. Sicily's seafaring traditions have given rise to complex yet tasty preserved foods such as botargo alla ventresca and bolzonaglia made from tuna or swordfish and preserved sardines. The cheeses are also excellent in Sicily and there are a number of local specialties (such as Vastedda and Maiorchino).

Citrus fruits and almonds top the list of dessert ingredients together with spices and candied fruits as well as the splendid local pistachio nuts, which were originally imported from the east. A few of the specialties include Cassata cheesecake, marzipan, Torroni nougat and gelato.

WHERE TO FIND SICILIAN SPECIALTIES IN ITALY

BOLOGNA	**MATUSEL:** Via Bertoloni, 2 - Tel.: 051 231718 **SIKELIA:** Via Riva di Reno 39/H - Tel.: 051 231551
BOLZANO	**RISTORANTE CORONA:** Via Streiter, 21 - Tel.: 0471 972624
CAGLIARI	**LE DUE ISOLE:** Via Enrico Pessina, 7/A - Tel.: 070 342188
FLORENCE	**LA TERRAZZA DEL PRINCIPE:** Viale Niccolò Machiavelli, 10 - Tel.: 055 2335375
GENOA	**TRATTORIA LE CAMMELLATE:** Corso Torino, 64/R - Tel.: 342 1459952
MILAN	**AL FICODINDIA:** Via Ruggero Bonghi, 11 - Tel.: 02 84892887 **OSTERIA MEDAGLIE D'ORO:** Piazza Medaglie D'Oro, 3 - Tel.: 02 55184023
PALERMO	**IL SICILIANO DOC:** Via Gaetano Filangeri, 10 - Tel.: 091 2525580 **RISTORANTE PIZZERIA TOSCA:** Via Pignatelli Aragona, 70 - Tel.: 091 584751 **TRATTORIA AI CASCINARI:** Via D'Ossuna, 43/45 - Tel.: 091 6519804
ROME	**CAPRICCI SICILIANI:** Via di Panico, 83 - Tel.: 06 45433823 **ISOLE DI SICILIA:** Via Garibaldi, 68 - Tel.: 06 58334212
TURIN	**A' VUCCIRIA:** Corso XI Febbraio, 7 - Tel.: 011 4361198 **EAT SICILY A PICCIRIDDA:** Via Vincenzo Bellini, 5 - Tel.: 011 537836
TRIESTE	**TRATTORIA ALLA SACCHETTA:** Riva Tommaso Gulli, 2 - Tel.: 040 300628
VENICE	**A BECCAFICO:** Campo S. Stefano, 2801 - Tel.: 041 5274879

APPETIZER

Arancini di riso

Arancini rice croquettes

TIME CONSUMING

AVERAGE

200g rice; 80g ground veal; 2 chicken giblets; 2 eggs; 150g green peas; 1 onion; 4 tablespoons tomato sauce; ½ litre meat broth; 4 tablespoons of grated Pecorino cheese; 40g butter; breadcrumbs, extra virgin olive oil, salt and pepper to taste.

These exceptional rice croquettes have a rich filling. They are very popular specialties they make a great way to start a meal.

PREPARATION

Brown the sliced onion in a little oil and butter. As soon as the onion begins to turn golden in colour, add the diced chicken giblets, the ground veal and the peas. Add salt, pepper and the tomato sauce and cook the mixture until the sauce thickens. Separately, cook the rice in broth (add the boiling broth a little at a time). Finally, add the remaining butter, the cheese, 1 egg and salt when the rice has finished cooking. Mix for a couple of minutes and allow the mixture to cool. When the rice has cooled use your hands to prepare 6 centimetre balls. Stuff the centre of the balls with the filling. Close the rice around the hole and seal it well. Dip the croquette in beaten egg, breadcrumbs and then deep fry. When the rice croquettes are golden brown on each side, set them on a paper towel to absorb any excess oil.

THE LOCAL PRODUCT

PECORINO SICILIANO CHEESE
Pecorino cheese is made with whole unpasteurized sheep milk in Sicily. The milk is set aside in a cool place after the evening milking and then it is added to the next morning's milk (or the milk from just one milking can be used). Pecorino Siciliano cheese is cylindrical in shape with flat slightly concave sides. It has a thin crust textured by the baskets it is formed in and a light golden colour that tends towards amber as it ages. The aroma is strong and pleasant. The fresh cheese has a mild flavour that becomes sharper and more savoury with age. There are also different varieties of Pecorino Siciliano cheese (including Tuma, Primo Sale and Secondo Sale) that have been aged for different amounts of times or have undergone different processing and ripening procedures. Another local specialty is "pipatu" which is made by adding whole black peppercorns (or occasionally dry red pepper flakes) when the cheese curd forms. It is great served plain or grated as a condiment.

MODERATE

AVERAGE

Pasta alla Norma

400g spaghetti; 2 eggplants; 500g tomato chunks or tomato sauce; 150g grated Ricotta Salata cheese; 2 garlic cloves; 1 onion; one bunch of fresh basil; extra virgin olive oil, salt and pepper to taste.

Eggplant is a wonderful and common ingredient in Sicilian cuisine. This pasta recipe is said to have developed in Catania as a tribute to composer Vincenzo Bellini and his famous "Norma". In truth it is just a variation on a common local pasta and eggplant theme. In this recipe the tomato and eggplant sauce blends with Ricotta Salata cheese perfectly.

PREPARATION

Cut the eggplant in ½ centimetre thick slices and place it in a pasta drainer and top it with salt. Set aside for one hour until the bitter juice drains out of the eggplant. In the meantime brown a diced onion, crushed garlic and a bunch of diced basil. After it browns, add the tomato and salt and cook over a low flame (uncovered) for half an hour and then top with olive oil. Rinse and dry the eggplant and fry it in oil. Drain the eggplant on paper towels. Cook the spaghetti in a large pot of salted water until it is al dente. Then top the pasta with the sauce and fried eggplant. Mix the ingredients, add crushed basil and pepper before serving.

THE LOCAL PRODUCT

MAMERTINO NERO D'AVOLA

Grapes have been growing on the slopes of Mt. Etna and around Agrigento since before the era of the Phoenicians according to some historians. Historical references to Mamertino wine production date back to 289 BC. Praised by Stradanus and Pliny, Mamertino was already considered one of the best wines sold even centuries ago. Mamertino Nero d'Avola and Nero d'Avola Riserva DOC wines are great with flavourful cheeses (like Sicilian pecorino or the traditional "piacintinu": sheep cheese aromatised with saffron). It is ideal with meat dishes such as veal ribs, or Messina-style kid goat.

FIRST COURSES

Pasta con le sarde

Pasta with Sardines

MODERATE

AVERAGE

350g short pasta; 300g cleaned sardines; 2 anchovy fillets; 2 level tablespoons of raisins softened in warm water; 30g pine nuts; 1 onion; 1g saffron; wild fennel, extra virgin olive oil, salt and pepper to taste.

Pasta with sardine sauce is another popular dish. It is famous for the perfect sweet and sour balance of the flavours – the wild fennel is an essential ingredient in this recipe.

PREPARATION

Remove the heads from the sardines and scrape off any scales. Slit the fish open and remove the backbones and entrails. Separately, boil the wild fennel in salted water for around 10 minutes and then dice it finely (set aside the water used to boil the fennel). Chop the sardines and brown them together with the sliced onions. Dissolve the saffron in a little warm water and then add it to the mixture along with the raisins, pine nuts, and diced fennel. Add a dash of salt and cook for 5 minutes (mixing) before adding the sardines and cooking the mixture another 5 minutes. Boil the pasta in the water set aside from the fennel. Cook the pasta until it is al dente. Top the pasta with the sauce and a dash of pepper.

THE LOCAL PRODUCT

RIESI DOC WINE

This DOC wine takes its name from the Riesi municipality in the Caltanissetta province, where the wine is produced in the central southern end of Sicily. The white pairs amazingly well with seafood specialties while the red accompanies red meats and flavourful cheeses. The rosé is great with pasta and sardines, appetizers and eggplant dishes. The spumante makes a fine aperitif and it is perfect with crustacean and seafood appetizers. Vendemmia Tardiva is a great dessert wine and it also pairs well with sharp cheeses, cookies and biscotti.

Baccalà in ghiotta

800g dried salted cod (soaked and skinned); 150g finely sliced onion; 250g well drained tomato chunks; 400g sliced potatoes; 150g pitted olives; 2 tablespoons of pine nuts; 2 tablespoons of raisins (soaked in warm water); 3 ripe pears; flour, extra virgin olive oil, salt and pepper to taste.

In Calabria and Sicily, the term "ghiotta" means a truly succulent and flavourful seafood dish. There are a number of variations, but most recipes include a blend of sweet and savoury flavours that is reminiscent of Middle Eastern culinary traditions. This unique and delicious codfish specialty is made with pears, raisins and pine nuts.

PREPARATION

Remove any bones and cut the codfish into pieces. Rinse and dry the codfish and then dip each piece in flour. Separately, boil the potatoes in salted water (they should still be firm and not mushy); dice the olives; peel, core and slice the pears. In a large pan brown the onion in a few tablespoons of oil and then brown the codfish on both sides before adding the tomato chunks and a little pepper. Check for salt and simmer for 8 minutes over a medium flame before adding the potatoes (and a little bit of the water they were cooked in), olives, pears, raisins and pine nuts. Cook for a couple of minutes so that the flavours blend. Serve hot.

THE LOCAL PRODUCT

PACHINO TOMATO
Pachino tomatoes are named for the town where they grow in the province of Siracusa. The area provides a perfect environment for the plant with a sunny exposition, the salinity of the irrigation water, the texture of the soil and the vicinity to the sea which helps keep the climate mild and almost eliminates any risk of winter or spring frost. These factors all contribute to the unique organoleptic qualities of Pachino tomatoes giving them a sweet taste, firm pulp and shiny skin - and they are long-lasting after they have been harvested. The first Pachino tomato farms date back to 1925 however they only started gaining national popularity in the 70s.

Farsumagro

TIME CONSUMING

DIFFICULT

1 thick veal steak (weight 800g); 3 hard boiled eggs (sliced); 4 slices of soft cheese; 50g prosciutto crudo cut into cubes; 2 garlic cloves (leave the skin on); 1 onion and 1 carrot (diced); 1 glass of white wine; 1 bay leaf; 3 tablespoons of diced garlic, oregano and parsley; extra virgin olive oil, salt and pepper to taste.

This stuffed steak roll is a classic holiday dish that is elaborate, flavourful and very hearty. It makes a perfect dish for an important occasion.

PREPARATION

Mix together the hard-boiled eggs, cheese, prosciutto and the diced mixture. Pound the meat flat and then place the egg mixture on top of the meat. Top with salt and pepper and then roll the meat tightly and tie it together with kitchen twine. Salt and pepper the outside of the meat and brush with oil before cooking it in an oiled baking pan with diced carrot, onion, two whole garlic cloves and the bay leaf. Add a little water and salt and then bake at 180° for around 1 hour (periodically basting the meat). After one hour remove the meat from the pan and allow it to cool. In the meantime add the wine to the drippings and cook over a high flame until the sauce thickens. Untie the meat and slice it. Place on a serving dish and cover with the sauce.

THE LOCAL PRODUCT

PICURINU AND RAGUSANO CHEESE Picurinu has been made the same way for so long that it is recognised as the oldest kind of cheese on the island. There are references to sheep milk cheese by Greek authors and then by Pliny the Elder in his Naturalis Historia. In Homer's Odyssey, the giant Polyphemus invents cheese and the tale even describes how the cheese was made: "They sat and took turns milking the sheep and the bleating goats. Then after returning the mothers to their lambs they made curd from half the milk and placed it in shining baskets". Ragusano is another of the oldest-known varieties of cheese in Sicily. It was originally known "caciocavallo" from Ragusa due to the fact that it was hung over a bar to dry, which gave it a characteristic caciocavallo shape. The first historical references to the cheese date back to the 14th century when it is cited as being a valuable commodity outside the Kingdom of Sicily in a number of different documents.

Caponata

This flavourful vegetable side dish is great and long lasting. Caponata is frequently confused with other recipes – this is the original recipe.

800g dark purple eggplant; 3 onions; 300g tomato chunks; 2 celery stalks; 100g pitted olives and capers; basil, vinegar, extra virgin olive oil, sugar and salt to taste

PREPARATION

Cut the eggplant into chunks, cover the chunks in salt and let them drain in a pasta strainer for at least one hour until all the bitter juices have been drawn out. In the meantime, brown the sliced onion in a little oil and after a few minutes add the tomato chunks, olives, capers and diced celery. Add salt and pepper and cook for 15 minutes. Rinse the eggplant and set it on a smooth towel to dry. Deep fry the eggplant until it turns golden in colour and then set it on a paper towel to remove any excess oil. Add the eggplant, ½ cup of vinegar and 1 teaspoon of sugar to the sauce. Mix and cook over a medium flame. When the sauce has thickened, turn off the stove, add the basil and stir. Serve cold.

THE LOCAL PRODUCT

CAPERS

Capers have been used since the time of the Greeks and the Romans and not only known for their culinary uses. They were used for their medicinal and even aphrodisiacal properties in Biblical times. In Greek and Latin capers were known by the Greek name kapparis, which probably had pre-Indo-European origins. Many writers including Hippocrates, Dioscorides, Pliny the Elder, and Galenus spoke of the aphrodisiac and cosmetic properties of capers while Apicius cited their culinary uses. The first references to the sale of capers produced in the French regions of Provence and Var date back to the seventeen hundreds.

DESSERT

Cannoli

TIME CONSUMING

AVERAGE

300g flour; 250g sugar; 500g ricotta; 25g candied fruits; 25g ground pistachio nuts; ½ glass of wine (Marsala wine if possible); dark chocolate slivers, vanilla, cinnamon, powdered sugar, extra virgin olive oil and salt to taste

Born as a Mardi gras treat, Sicilian cannoli are round tubes of crispy pastry filled with ricotta and other delights. They are truly amazing right after they have been filled. These goodies offer a nice sampling of local ingredients with ricotta, candied fruits and pistachio nuts.

PREPARATION

Mix together the flour, wine, 1 level tablespoon of sugar and a pinch of salt and knead the mixture until it forms a firm dough. Cover the dough and set it aside for a couple of hours. In the meantime, mix together the ricotta, candied fruits, chocolate slivers, sugar, one pinch of vanilla and one pinch of cinnamon. Roll out a thin crust and cut it into 10-centimetre squares. Wrap each piece of dough around a metal cannoli form and deep fry it. Remove the cannoli as soon as they turn golden in colour and drain them on a paper towel. Before they have cooled completely, remove the metal cannoli form. Right before serving, stuff the cannoli with the filling and dip the edges in ground pistachio nuts and powdered sugar. It is important to fill them right before you are ready to eat them because otherwise the filling makes the crust soggy.

THE LOCAL PRODUCT

THE PISTACHIO FROM BRONTE

Some scholars believe that the pistachio originated in Syria while others claim it originated in Asia Minor or Turkestan. The pistachio was well known in past times and the pistachio nut is even cited in Genesis as one of the gifts sent to the pharaoh in 1802 BC: "Take a little balm, a little honey, gum, myrrh, pistachio nuts and almonds". The Arabs conquered Sicily after Byzantium and they brought the pistachio to the island. Cultivation spread in the Caltanissetta, Agrigento and Catania provinces at the end of the eighteen hundreds. In Catania at the foot of Mt. Etna in the Bronte area, entire pastures and fields were planted with pistachio trees, which would grow to become the focus of the entire agricultural and economic system in the area.

Cassata (which derives from the Arab word "Quas'at" meaning a large round bowl), is a Sicilian layered cake specialty from Palermo and it occupies a place of honour on the list of regional desserts. In past times Cassata was generally eaten on Easter after Lent was over, but these days it is a specialty all year long.

MODERATE

DIFFICULT

DESSERT

Cassata

Cassata Cake

1 sponge cake; 1 glass of white vermouth;
For the marzipan: 200ml water, green food colouring; 200g of almond flour; 1 vanilla sachet; 200g sugar
For the filling: 1 teaspoon of cinnamon; 100g dark chocolate slivers; 100g of candied fruit (in chunks); 50g of blanched pistachio nuts; 800g of sheep ricotta cheese; 3 tablespoons of rum; 2 vanilla sachets; 500g powdered sugar
For the icing: orange flower extract and powdered sugar to taste

PREPARATION

Use a wooden spoon to mix the fresh ricotta together with the powdered sugar, one vanilla sachet, cinnamon and rum. Continue mixing until it is smooth and creamy. Add the chocolate slivers, pistachio nuts and the candied fruit cut into chunks.
Prepare the green marzipan: Boil 200g of sugar and 200g of water until the sugar begins to form strings. Then add 200g of almond flour, green food colouring and a sachet of vanilla. Mix until smooth and then pour the mixture onto a moistened stone dough board. As soon as it has cooled, knead the marzipan until it is smooth and compact. Make a syrup from orange flower extract, powdered sugar and water. Roll out a thin sheet of marzipan. Cut the sponge cake horizontally to create four round disks. Oil a round 21cm diameter baking pan with high sides and lay the sheet of marzipan onto the pan. Place one of the layers of sponge cake on top of the marzipan. Top the cake with a swirl of orange flower syrup and a layer of ricotta filling. Repeat this process with all four layers of sponge cake (with the cake layer on the top) and then refrigerate the cake so that the filling can thicken. When the cake is cool remove it from the refrigerator, turn the mould upside down onto a plate and then top the cake with a glaze made from orange flower extract, powdered sugar and a tiny bit of water. Top the cake with candied fruits

TUSCANY

Florentine meat is not only beefsteak, we also find Scottiglia, which is a rich meat stew that originated in the mountains and is eaten throughout Tuscany. It contains a mixture of different meats (depending on what is available) including beef, pork, rabbit, chicken, duck, game and lamb. The meats are boiled for a few hours with broth, red wine, tomatoes and herbs. The dish is hearty with an intense flavour and the meat is extraordinarily tender.

We must also mention the delicious wild boar specialties throughout the region, which are celebrated at a weeklong festival in Suvereto in the Florence province at the beginning of December. We also find high quality pork (including a native variety called Cinta Senese) which is used to make amazing salamis (like finocchiona in the Chianti zone, the rarer mortadella from Prato and a number of variations on sanguinaccio as well as Lardo di Colonnata). Among the pork specialties we find a rare specialty that is worth a mention called Tonno di Chianti or Tuna from Chianti. This dish is actually suckling pork thigh that has been salted and aromatized with rosemary before being boiled in white wine. After cooking it is preserved under oil and the end result is a truly tender delicacy.

Though not very widespread, Zeri lambs are quite a specialty in the Lunigana area. One of the last breeds to still be raised out in the open as a wild animal, it has aromatic and tender meat with a delicious flavour.

After this long description of meats, we have said very little about Tuscan specialties which also include fine olive oil, internationally famous wine, great vegetables (like zolfino beans), mushrooms (Mount Abetone and Amiata are great for mushrooms) excellent cheeses, tasty desserts, savoury stews and seafood specialties.

WHERE TO FIND TUSCAN SPECIALTIES IN ITALY

BOLOGNA	**RISTORANTE 7 ARCHI:** Via Marchesana, 6 - Tel.: 051 233227 **TRATTORIA AI BUTTERI:** Via Augusto Murri, 20 - Tel.: 051 347718
CAGLIARI	**NUOVO ROYAL:** Via Bottego, 24 - Tel.: 070 341313
FLORENCE	**OSTERIA I RIFFAIOLI:** Via del Ponte alle Riffe, 2-4/R - Tel.: 055 5088070 **TRATTORIA DALL'OSTE:** Via Luigi Alamanni, 3/5 - Tel.: 055 212048 **TRATTORIA NELLA:** Via delle Terme 19/R - Tel.: 055 218925
GENOA	**LA TORRE DEL MANGIA:** Piazza Nicolò Montano, 24 - Tel.: 010 465607
MILAN	**CASA TUA OSTERIA:** Via Benedetto Corio, 3 - Tel.: 02 5514269 **TRATTORIA TORRE DI PISA:** Via Fiori Chiari, 21/5 - Tel.: 02 874877
NAPLES	**I BISCHERI:** Via Cimarosa, 26/28 - Tel.: 081 19575736 **MAREMMA MAIALA:** Riviera di Chiaia, 270 - Tel.: 081 7642262
PALERMO	**PASSIONE IN CUCINA:** Via G. Turrisi Colonna, 10 - Tel.: 091 582443
ROME	**LA FIORENTINA:** Via Andrea Doria, 22 - Tel.: 06 39737019 **LA MORA:** Piazza Crati, 13 - Tel.: 06 86206613
TURIN	**CHE BOLLE IN PENTOLA?:** Via Rivara, 30 - Tel.: 011 7930961 **TRATTORIA IVO 1958:** Corso Novara, 75 - Tel.: 011 852806
TRIESTE	**AL TOSCANO:** Via Bonomea, 114 - Tel.: 040 425057
VENICE	**DA IVO:** Calle dei Fuseri, 1809 - Tel.: 041 5285004

APPETIZER

Crostino toscano

MODERATE

EASY

2 chicken livers (remove veins, fat and bits of green bile); 200g skinned spleen; 8 thin slices of dry unsalted bread; 2 anchovy fillets; 1 tablespoon of flour; 1 tablespoon of diced capers; 30g of butter; diced parsley, salt and pepper to taste

Fragrant toasted bread topped with liver pâté - a magnificent Tuscan specialty. This is a typical starter at any fine local restaurant.

PREPARATION

Chop the livers and spleen very finely and brown them in butter. Add a dash of salt and chopped parsley, anchovies and capers as well as salt and pepper, flour and a couple of tablespoons of water. Cook the mixture while stirring constantly. Toast the slices of bread and top with the sauce. Serve cold or hot.

THE LOCAL PRODUCT

TUSCAN BREAD

White bread in Tuscany has been around since the imperial era and it is made from soft grain wheat that is grown throughout the area giving the bread special characteristics. In time, Tuscan bakers began using a mixture of soft grains that were grown locally as well as wild yeasts and sourdough for leavening. The flour is mixed with sourdough and warm water in the following proportions: 7 parts flour, 3 parts sourdough. The dough is kneaded for a long time and then it is set aside to rise for several hours. The dough is formed into long oval or round loaves that weigh ½ kilo or more after they have been baked. The surface of the loaf is cut before being baked in the oven. Tuscan bread is made without salt and therefore it is best when paired with something savoury such as the flavourful local cheese or salami. A number of Tuscan specialties are made from bread including soups and stews like the famous Ribollita, or bruschetta (also known as Fettunte) topped with olive oil and even bread salads like Panzanella.

MODERATE

EASY

Acquacotta

1 medium onion, 1 carrot and 1 stalk of celery cut finely; 1 bell pepper (remove the seeds and core and cut into strips); 1 clove of garlic; 4 tablespoons of extra virgin olive oil; 150g of canned tomatoes cut in slices; 4 slices of dry hard grain bread (cut in half), one small red pepper

Famous for its simplicity, the name of this dish actually means 'cooked water'. It was a common dish for those who worked far from home and all it required was a wood fire, a pot of water and whatever vegetables or herbs the land offered. The choice of ingredients varied a great deal depending on where it was made and the season. A somewhat standard recipe evolved over the years, but there are still a number of variations in the ingredients.

PREPARATION

Brown the carrot, celery and garlic in a little oil and then add the tomatoes, bell pepper and red pepper. Cook for ten minutes mixing occasionally. Add 1½ litre of broth and salt and boil for 20 minutes. In the meantime place the bread in the bowls, pour the soup over the top and serve. You can also add finely sliced grilled porcini mushrooms and/or a beaten egg and grated pecorino cheese.

THE LOCAL PRODUCT

OLIVE OIL FROM CHIANTI

Oil cultivation in this area has ancient roots and it prospered for nutritional and even religious reasons (certain rituals and ceremonies required the use of oil). The production area was recognized in 1716 with an edict by Duke Cosimo III who recognized the quality of the oil and wine made within the current-day Chianti Classico production area.

MODERATE

EASY

FIRST COURSES

TUSCANY

Pappa col pomodoro

4 slices of dry hard grain bread;
400g tomato chunks; 2 garlic cloves;
½ an onion; 1 celery stalk; basil,
extra virgin olive oil, salt and pepper to taste.

This is another dish where stale bread is turned into a bread soup delight. Strongly linked to rural farm traditions, this dish is always a success.

PREPARATION

Dice the onion, celery and garlic and brown the mixture in a little oil. Add the tomato chunks, one cup of water and salt and pepper then simmer for 20 minutes. Add the bread (break it into chunks) and basil and continue cooking for another 20 minutes. Top with olive oil before serving.

THE LOCAL PRODUCT

ROSSO DI MONTEPULCIANO WINE This wine is produced in Montepulciano in the Siena province. There are many historical references that praise the excellent wine. It was praised as "the king of all wines" in a Tuscan poem written in 1685 by Francesco Redi (a famous physician and naturalist). His words resounded far and wide and made Montepulciano wine famous even outside Italy. It was one of William III of England's favourite wines. Recently classified as a DOC wine together with Vino Nobile di Montepulciano, (which in actuality is the same wine but it is made with different production parameters including the amount of grapes produced per hectare, the alcohol content and the aging process). It pairs well with appetizers, soups, pasta with meat sauce, game, white and red meats, legumes and flavourful cheeses.

TIME CONSUMING

AVERAGE

Ribollita

8 slices of dry hard grain bread sliced in half; 200g fresh cannellini or white beans (or dry beans that have been soaked); 300g of each of the following washed and cut into strips: cabbage (green or Savoy) and Kale (Dinosaur Kale if possible); 500g of Swiss chard; 250g tomato chunks; 1 potato (peeled and cut into chunks); ½ an onion, 1 garlic clove and 1 stalk of celery; 200g of pork rind or prosciutto cut into strips; thyme; diced parsley, extra virgin olive oil, salt and pepper to taste.

This extremely popular bread soup recipe is named for the way it is cooked. In Italian 'bollita' means boiled and 'ribollita' means re-boiled. After the soup has finished cooking, it is set aside for a few hours so that the flavours blend. Then it is topped with olive oil and brought back up to a boil before serving.

PREPARATION

Boil the beans in 1½ litres of salted water and make sure that they remain covered with water the whole time they are cooking (if needed add hot water). Boil until the beans are soft but not mushy. In the meantime dice the onion, garlic, celery, thyme and parsley very finely. Brown the mixture and then add the vegetables (first the cabbage and kale and then the Swiss chard and the potato). Add salt and pepper and the tomato chunks and simmer (add a ladleful of water from the beans if the mixture becomes too dry). Add around ¼ of the beans to the vegetables. Puree the other beans and the broth and then add the pureed mixture to the vegetable mixture. Line a sauce pan or double boiler with two layers of bread. Cover the bread with the vegetables and broth. Repeat with another two layers of bread and a layer of broth (set aside a little of the broth to add after the bread has soaked up all the broth). After the bread has soaked up all the liquid, add the remaining broth. The next day cook the pan over a very low flame and top with olive oil, salt and pepper and simmer slowly (taking care that it does not stick) for 5 minutes.

THE LOCAL PRODUCT

PROSCIUTTO FROM TUSCANY

During the 15th century (the era of the Medici dynasty) the entire process for the production of Prosciutto was regulated by law in Tuscany and it is still made the very same way today. Prosciutto has its roots in ancient farm traditions in Tuscany. Pigs were slaughtered in the winter after having fattened for one year and then the pork was transformed into charcuterie products for family consumption. As agriculture evolved, artisan processing centres and small industries developed but the timeworn processing traditions and traditional product characteristics have stayed the same.

Caciucco

MODERATE

AVERAGE

350g cleaned cuttlefish; 350g cleaned octopus; 200g dogfish; 300g fish for soup stock (such as Sea Robin, Tub Gurnard or Scorpion fish); 300g of mixed seafood (clams and mussels); 300g crustaceans (large and small shrimp, scampi, spiny lobster); 8 slices of dry hard grain bread (toasted and topped with pepper and garlic); 1 cup of tomato sauce; white wine, garlic, sage, red pepper, extra virgin olive oil, salt and pepper to taste

Few dishes have been transformed through the ages like this rich seafood specialty. The original recipe was prepared and served to the prisoners who rowed ships (chained to the oars). The recipe has been simplified over time and now it contains fewer but higher quality varieties of fish.

PREPARATION

In a Dutch oven, brown the garlic, sage and diced red pepper. Add the octopus and cuttlefish (cut into pieces) and simmer for a couple of minutes before adding the white wine. Then add the tomato sauce and check for salt and pepper. Cook for 20 minutes mixing occasionally. Add the soup fish and the dogfish and continue cooking over a medium flame. When the octopus and sepia are tender, add the crustaceans, clams and mussels. Continue cooking for 6-7 minutes until the clams and mussels open. Toasted garlic bread should be placed on the bottom of each bowl and topped with fish and sauce.

THE LOCAL PRODUCT

CHIANTI The first document that mentions Chianti was written in 1398. Later, the wine was perfected and it became a favourite of Pope Paul in 1536. In 1713 Cosimo III the Grand Duke of Tuscany issued two decrees regarding Chianti. The first established the best Chianti production areas and the second was a sort of guideline for making it. However, that was still not modern Chianti, which was developed by Baron Bettino Ricasoli who tried a number of different grape blends before settling on a final choice that is the Chianti we know and love today. Several sub-regions produce Chianti wines with slightly different characteristics.

1 kilo of mullet (cleaned); 2 garlic cloves and a handful of diced parsley; 1 red pepper; 500g tomato sauce; flour, extra virgin olive oil and salt to taste.

Triglie alla livornese

Livorno-style Mullet

This popular dish is one of the best mullet recipes around and the aromatic filling is the key to this recipe's success.

PREPARATION

Stuff the belly of each mullet with diced parsley and garlic and then dip the fish in flour. Brown the fish on both sides in a little oil and red pepper (be careful when turning it so that the herbs do not fall out). Add the tomato sauce and the remaining diced parsley and garlic. Check for salt and cook over a high flame until the sauce has thickened. Serve hot from the pan (remove the hot pepper). This dish can also be prepared by cooking the tomatoes first and then adding the mullet (without frying or breading it).

THE LOCAL PRODUCT

VERNACCIA

This wine is only produced in the municipality of San Gimignano. According to the most likely story, Vernaccia takes its name from the Latin term "vernaculum" which means native. This etymological interpretation explains why many grape varieties in Italy are named with this same name. This wine has been made in the area for a very long time and written references to it date back to the 13th century. It was also the first white Tuscan wine to ever receive DOC classification. It is great with seafood (especially crustaceans), fried dishes, egg dishes, white meats and salami.

MODERATE

EASY

Fagioli all'uccelletto

700g shelled white beans; 1 cup tomato sauce; 1 crushed garlic clove; 2 sage leaves; extra virgin olive oil, ground pepper and salt to taste.

This land is famous for several white bean varieties such as the famous Zolfino or the rarer Sorana bean and Tuscany uses white beans a great deal in soups. Beans are the protagonist of two well known recipes including 'fagioli al fiasco' and this recipe for flavourful beans in a sage and tomato sauce.

PREPARATION

Cook the beans in salted water for 20 minutes. In the meantime, brown the oil, garlic and sage. Drain the beans and add to the pan and cook for a few minutes before adding the tomato sauce and a cup of warm water. Check for salt and cook over a low flame for 20 minutes. Before serving add a dash of fresh ground pepper

THE LOCAL PRODUCT

SORANA BEANS

Sorana beans are very different than other varieties of cannellini beans due to their different taste, smaller size and diverse shape (the white bean is almost flat, the red is cylindrical with a slightly thicker skin) and the extremely soft skin that almost seems to melt in your mouth. It is a white bean with pearly veining or there is a red variety with darker veining and both have an exquisite and delicate flavour. The Sorana bean was mentioned by Gioacchino Rossini (who was a great fan) in a letter to his friend Giovanni Pacini where he expressly requested the legume as payment for revising a few scores.

MODERATE

EASY

Castagnaccio

300g chestnut flour; 2 tablespoons of sugar; 20g of raisins soaked in warm water; 20g pine nuts; rosemary, fennel seeds, extra virgin olive oil and salt to taste.

This was a simple farm dessert that called for few ingredients that were available locally. Chestnut flour was used as a primary staple in the poorer mountain areas.

PREPARATION

Mix together the flour, sugar, salt and warm water to create a firm dough. Knead the dough until it is smooth and there are no lumps and then add the fennel seeds. Oil the pan, press the dough into the pan until it is about 2 finger-widths in height. Top with raisins, pine nuts and rosemary and then brush with a little oil and bake in a preheated oven at 200° Celsius. Bake for 40 minutes or until the top is golden brown. Cool before serving.

THE LOCAL PRODUCT

NECCIO DELLA GARFAGNANA CHESTNUT FLOUR

It is made in the Lucca province surrounding Garfagnana. The chestnut flour is a white or dark ivory colour with a sweet taste and a slightly bitter aftertaste. It is very fine to the touch and on the tongue. After being harvested, the chestnuts are carried to the 'metato' (a two-storey structure used for drying them). Thanks the heat and smoke of a wood fire burning on the ground floor of the metato, the chestnuts on the floor above (spread out on cloths), dry in about 40 days. After drying, they are shelled, selected and stone-ground so that the flour does not lose any of its special organoleptic characteristics..

TRENTINO ALTO ADIGE

When climbing up the Adriatic coast after crossing the plains and hills, we meet the first mountains. The domain of the Alps begins here with peaks and valleys, forests and waterways that outline the perimeter of the land. This beautiful landscape has a rich traditional culture shared by two areas: Trentino and Alto Adige. These two different and similar lands are linked not only by their proximity. The Chiusa di Salorno is a natural bottleneck and passageway along the Adige mountains from the south and it marks the border between the southern section of the region (Trentino which is similar to Venice in its culture and traditions), and the northern section (Alto Adige or South Tyrol which is more closely linked to Austrian culture and traditions). The local food highlights this regional duplicity and in some ways it highlights the nearness of these people who have always shared the same mountains.

In Trentino we find strong flavours and lots of polenta dishes which originated in Veneto. In the Alto Adige area we find more delicate sweet and sour flavours as well as the extensive use of buckwheat and rye flour, which derive from Austrian and Hungarian influences.

However, both of the areas have developed many preserved foods (incredible salami such as mortandela or speck, and salt-cured meats as well as sauerkraut, jams, syrups and distillates) and incredible dairy specialties (great cheeses including Puzzone di Moena or Pergler). We find apples in both areas (in Val di Non and Val Venosta) and vineyards in the valleys (that produce famous wines and spumanti) as well as berries, mushrooms and wild game. Though they do not share the same history, the people of both areas are united by the mountains which provide them the same natural stimuli and resources.

The result of these two cultures blending has given rise to absolutely excellent cuisine. Discovering the specialties from Trento and Alto Adige provides a treasured occasion for tasting the best the Alps has to offer with an extraordinary variety of flavours.

WHERE TO FIND TRENTINO AND ALTO ADIGE SPECIALTIES IN ITALY

BOLOGNA	**CHIARO DI LUNA - MONDSCHEIN:** Via Andrea Costa, 34/D - Tel.: 051 433701
BOLZANO	**CAVALLINO BIANCO:** Via Bottai, 6 - Tel.: 0471 973267 **PAULANER STUBEN:** Via Argentieri, 16 - Tel.: 0471 980407 **RISTORANTE KAISERKRON:** Piazza della Mostra, 2 - Tel.: 0471 980214
CAMPOBASSO	**BIER KELLER:** Vico Percettore, 9 - Tel.: 0874 311406
GENOA	**BIRRERIA HOFBRÄUHAUS:** Via Boccardo, 5R - Tel.: 010 542988 **CATTIVI CONSIGLI:** Piazza Duca Degli Abruzzi, 2 - Tel.: 010 3726062
MILAN	**TAVERNA DELLA TRISA:** Via Ferruccio, 1 - Tel.: 02 341304
ROME	**CANTINA TIROLESE:** Via Giovanni Vitelleschi, 23 - Tel.: 06 68135297
TRENTO	**RISTORANTE LOTO:** Via Gocciadoro, 62 - Tel.: 0461 917190 **TRATTORIA LA BUCA DI BACCO:** Via dei Ventuno, 1 - Tel.: 0461 983161 **TRATTORIA LA STUA:** Via dei Mille, 22 - Tel.: 0461 915879
TRIESTE	**BIRRERIA FORST:** Via Giorgio Galatti, 11 - Tel.: 040 363486 **BUFFET DA PEPI:** Via Cassa di Risparmio, 3 - Tel.: 040 366858 **KAPUZINER KELLER:** Via Pozzo del Mare, 1 - Tel.: 040 307997

Canederli

Canederli Dumplings

MODERATE

AVERAGE

500g rye bread; ½ cup of milk; 2 eggs; 1bunch of parsley; 30g butter; 250g smoked meat (or speck); 1 litre of meat broth; Trentigrana or Parmesan cheese, salt and pepper to taste

These tasty dumplings are probably the best known and most popular specialty from Trento. A very hearty and filling dish, it is definitely suited to autumn and winter menus.

PREPARATION

Mix the bread (cut into chunks), milk, diced parsley, salt, pepper and 2 eggs. Use your hands to blend the mixture well and then form small round dumplings and cook them in broth for 10 minutes. Serve the dumplings and broth piping hot with grated cheese and melted butter.

THE LOCAL PRODUCT

TRENTINGRANA CHEESE

Trentigrana cheese belongs to the Consortium for the Protection of Grana Padano Cheese and Trentigrana is made the same way as Grana Padano (the only difference is that it is made in Trentino). This hard cheese is aged slowly (at least 18-20 months) and it is highly nutritious. The crust is firm, tight, shiny and almost brown. The cheese is grainy and friable. The delicate fragrant flavour makes it perfect for topping vegetable and bean dishes, polenta, rice, pasta and salads. It is also great plain to start or end a meal.

Minestrone d'orzo
Barley Soup

150g barley; 80g speck ham cut into strips; 160g smoked meat; diced mixture: onion, carrot, celery and leeks; 50g of dry beans soaked for 12 hours; 2 peeled potatoes cut into chunks; butter and salt to taste

TIME CONSUMING

EASY

This magnificent barley soup from Alto Adige makes a complete meal that is soothing and long-lasting – it makes a perfect wintertime specialty.

PREPARATION

Lightly brown the ham in butter. Add the diced mixture and the smoked meat and cook until it is golden brown. Pour in 1½ litre of hot salted water and simmer the mixture for 1 hour over a low flame. Then add the potatoes, barley and beans, check the salt and continue cooking for another 30 minutes. Remove the smoked meat, dice it and then place it back in the pan. Cook over a medium flame for a minute so that the flavours can blend and then serve.

THE LOCAL PRODUCT

SPECK FROM ALTO ADIGE

The first historical references to Alto Adige Speck (salt-cured, smoked juniper-flavoured ham) date back to the beginning of the 1300s when the very same production techniques were used to make a product called "bachen". Sources from Alto Adige refer to the product as Lardum and it was included in part of the Butcher's Regulations in Trento in 1307 in a law stating that salted meat, speck, cheese, oil and lard sellers should not cheat on weights. In a document from 1381 we find that speck was hung in the attic and not aged in the cellar, because it was better for developing the fragrance. The term speck in modern Italian replaced the older term (bachen) at the beginning of the 18th century. One of the first references to speck in 1785 refers to smoked speck, so most likely at that time speck only referred to the cut of pork and not the treatment. For the first decade of the twentieth century, farmers would go to cities for Sunday mass with a piece of speck that the innkeeper (or even the parish priest) would boil and then distribute at the end of mass. At times they would even leave a small offering to repay his efforts.

Gulasch

Goulash

TIME CONSUMING

AVERAGE

700g beef cut into pieces; 3 diced onions; 1 glass of full-bodied red wine; the zest of 1 lemon; 1 teaspoon of paprika; 1 cup of tomato sauce; 1 garlic clove, bay leaves, rosemary, marjoram, flour, extra virgin olive oil, salt and pepper to taste.

Though it originated in Austria and Hungary, goulash is a very common specialty in Alto Adige as well as nearby areas. Rich in flavours, it makes a great base for creative additions. This recipe is the traditional version in Val Pusteria and it has a fine balance of flavours.

PREPARATION

Brown the meat and onion in a pan with a little oil. In the meantime mix the paprika and one teaspoon of flour in a glass of water and pour it over the meat, then add the wine and cook until the sauce thickens. Then add the herbs, lemon, salt and pepper and tomato sauce. Cover and cook over a low flame for at least two hours. Add a little water if necessary.

THE LOCAL PRODUCT

TEROLDEGO ROTALIANO WINE

The grapes are grown in a sandy valley that lies north of the point where the Adige and Noce Rivers meet. The wine takes its name from the grape which originated in the province. It is defined as the prince of wines of Trentino and it was cited in the chronicles of the Council of Trent in 1673. According to local evidence, Teroldego grapes were cultivated all the way back to 200 BC. The red pairs well with red meats, game, kid goat, boiled meats, polenta and flavourful cheeses. The 'superior' wine is ideal with grana cheese and Tyrol-style chamois. The rosato is best with barley soup, first courses with delicate toppings, mild salami, white meats, fresh cheeses and omelettes.

TIME CONSUMING

EASY

Crauti

Sauerkraut

1 kilo of green cabbage (cleaned); saffron, cumin, pepper, juniper berries and salt to taste

This German dish is popular all over the world and in particular in this region of Italy and Alto Adige. It can be purchased in local shops where it is made in wooden tubs or it can be made at home with the recipe below.

PREPARATION

Rinse and drain the cabbage well and then cut it into very fine strips and allow it to dry a little (squeeze it to remove excess moisture). Place the cabbage in a ceramic container with alternating layers of spices and salt. Allow the sauerkraut to ferment for two months: the sauerkraut produces brine that preserves it. Fermented sauerkraut should be washed to remove any excess salt before it is eaten. After squeezing the sauerkraut to remove any excess water, it is cooked with onion, carrot, smoked bacon, pepper and juniper berries as well as broth and white wine. In past times, people also added goose fat or pork lard. Cook for 3-4 hours. The dish can be eaten alone or accompanied by smoked cold cuts.

THE LOCAL PRODUCT

ALTO ADIGE – SÜDTIROL WINE

This DOC wine is made from grapes that grow along the banks of the Adige River in 34 municipalities in Bolzano. The area has great conditions for grapes and one of the oldest wine traditions in Europe. It was started by the Etruscans and later consolidated by the Romans. There are a number of varieties available including red, white and rosé specialties.

DESSERT

Krapfen

Rye Doughnuts

TIME CONSUMING

AVERAGE

400g rye flour; 25g brewer's yeast; 80g butter; 1 egg yolk; 2 tablespoons of cream; 3 tablespoons of red currants (fresh or frozen); 2 peeled apples; milk, breadcrumbs, rendered lard; powdered sugar and salt to taste

Krapfen (doughnuts) are popular throughout the world and it must be said that this specialty can be prepared in a number of ways. This particular recipe highlights the bounty of the local fruit.

PREPARATION

Mix the warmed butter and the flour with the cream, some of the milk an egg yolk and a pinch of salt. Dissolve the brewer's yeast in the milk and mix it into the dough. Mix well until the dough is smooth then cover it and set it aside for 1 hour. In the meantime, grate the apple and then mix it with the currants and breadcrumbs. Roll out a very thin sheet of dough and cut out 8-centimeter disks and place a spoonful of the filling at the centre of each one and then close it by folding the dough over onto itself and pressing well along the border. Heat the lard in a large pan and fry the doughnuts a few at a time until they are golden brown on both sides. Drain on paper towels, top with powdered sugar and serve hot.

THE LOCAL PRODUCT

CASTELLER WINE

The production area runs from the edge of Veneto across Trentino to the edge of Alto Adige. The vineyards are cultivated in the valley and on hills at 600 metres above sea level. The wine is made from native Schiava grapes (both "grossa" and "gentile" varieties) and it was already quite popular in the 1800s. It pairs well with soups, ravioli, cannelloni, speck, brioldi (sausage) with sauerkraut, white and red meats, omelettes, salami, soft cheeses, rabbit and plums. The amabile version is ideal with fruit pies, fruit cakes and Brazadel pound cake from Trento

TIME CONSUMING

DIFFICULT

DESSERT

Strudel di mele

Apple Strudel

200g flour; 1 large baking apple (peeled, cored and sliced finely); 120g raisins soaked in warm water; 60g pine nuts; 60g sugar; 1 shot of rum; 40g of breadcrumbs; 50g of butter; cinnamon and clove powder, powdered sugar, extra virgin olive oil and salt to taste.

This is the flagship recipe for Austrian-Hungarian inspired specialties. The word strudel actually means swirl and it is literally a swirled pastry with apples. There are a number of simpler variations and this version from Alto Adige may be laborious, but the results are well worth the extra effort.

PREPARATION

Mix the flour with 2 tablespoons of oil, a little salt and warm water. Knead well until the dough is smooth and firm. Divide the dough into two parts, brush with oil, cover and set aside for 1 hour. In the meantime mix the apples with the raisins, pine nuts, sugar, rum, a pinch of cinnamon and cloves. Roll out two square thin sheets of dough and place them on a smooth clean dish towel. Brown the breadcrumbs in butter until they are golden. When the breadcrumbs cooled, sprinkle them on top the dough (leave an empty space about 3 centimetres along one of the edges to seal the strudel). Spread the apple filling over the grated bread crumbs. Roll the strudel up (from the end without the empty space) and then press gently on the oiled edge to seal it. Butter a large baking pan and lay the two strudels onto it separately. Brush with melted butter and bake at 200° Celsius for 40 minutes or until they are golden brown. Top with powdered sugar and serve.

THE LOCAL PRODUCT

VAL DI NON APPLES:
DOP apples from Val Di Non include Golden Delicious, Renette Canada and Red Delicious varieties. The Golden delicious apples have a conical oblong shape with a colour ranging from green to yellow with pinkish highlights at times. The Red Delicious has an intense red colour over an intense green background while the Renetta Canada variety has a conical or flattened shape with a rough yellow-greenish hue. The Golden Delicious is crispy and succulent with a special sweet and sour flavour. The red delicious has a softer pulp with a sweetish taste. The Renetta Canada has a different texture and flavour depending on when it is eaten – it ranges from crisp and quite tart to softer and sweeter.

UMBRIA

Umbria is a small region with truly delightful cuisine and a number of local specialties including truffles. White truffles are found near Città di Castello and the more famous local black truffle is plentiful around Norcia and Spoleto. Both are celebrated at town festivals that take place during the first week in November (in Città di Castello) and during the second half of February in Norcia.

Norcia has a number of good reasons to celebrate food: the area's proverbial talent for processing pork gave rise to the Italian term "norcini" which is used to refer to all charcuterie specialties. The most famous of these is Corallina, which is long salami, made from fine cuts of meat seasoned with garlic and wine and aged for a few months. It is generally served on Easter Day. Another excellent specialty is the Porchetta (roasted pork with herbs and stuffing) – which some people say originated here. The specialty has been celebrated for over thirty years in Costano near Bastia Umbria on the second Sunday of September. Another lesser known specialty is Mazzafegato – salami made from pork liver in two varieties (mild honey or hot red pepper) and we cannot forget the sausage (the key ingredient for pasta alla norcina), guanciale, lard and prosciutto. They all pair well with another specialty from this plentiful land: the famous lentil from Castelluccio, which is small and tender enough that it does not have to be soaked and yet firm enough that it doesn't fall apart when cooking. The variety has been around since antiquity and it was a favourite of Cato the Elder who wrote down the first recipes for preparing them. In the middle of June when the lentils are in flower, Norcia pays tribute with a celebration to these lentils which have become increasingly popular in recent years.

Another local product that is quickly gaining popularity is Umbrian Caciotta cheese and Farro, a traditional grain which grows well here and is used in a number of delicious soups.

The local olive oil is excellent and the wines are gaining popularity. The culinary traditions in Umbria are rural and simple yet creative and incredibly satisfying.

WHERE TO FIND UMBRIAN SPECIALTIES IN ITALY

BOLOGNA

DAL BIASSANOT: Via Piella 16/A - Tel.: 051 230644
RISTORANTE CESOIA: Via Giuseppe Massarenti, 90 - Tel.: 051 342854
TRATTORIA IL TARTUFO: Via del Porto, 34 - Tel.: 051 252662

PERUGIA

DA CESARINO: Piazza IV Novembre, 5 - Tel.: 075 5728974
IL CASTELLO DELL'OCA: Strada Pievaiola, 283 - Tel.: 075 5293469
RISTORANTE RUBBAGALLINE: Via Elce Sotto, 21/23 - Tel.: 075 5735573

ROME

CUORE DELL'UMBRIA: Via Francesco d'Ovidio, 151 - Tel.: 06 45424617
LA TAVERNETTA: Viale Giulio Cesare, 103 - Tel.: 06 3214647
SEMIDIVINO: Via Alessandria, 230 - Tel.: 06 89016293

TURIN

RISTORANTE TEFY: Corso Belgio, 26 - Tel.: 011 837332
TAVERNA UMBRA: Via Buniva, 4/I - Tel.: 011 19702328

APPETIZER

Crostini al tartufo

Truffle Crostini

QUICK

EASY

6 slices of Italian bread; 100g of sliced truffles or truffle pate; 1 garlic clove; extra virgin olive oil, anchovy fillets, salt and pepper to taste.

This extremely simple appetizer of toasted bread and truffle pate is incredibly delicious thanks to the truffle. As in all simple recipes, the merit goes to the excellence of the ingredients.

PREPARATION

Dice the truffles and anchovy fillets (base the number of anchovies on your own personal taste) and mix them with olive oil. Toast the slices of bread (they are even better if they are grilled over a fire) and then spread the sauce over the top. It makes an amazing appetizer.

THE LOCAL PRODUCT

BLACK TRUFFLES

Umbria is well known for its truffles and the region produces around 100 tonnes each year. Experts say the region is like a giant natural truffle bed. In fact, 80% of Italian truffles are processed and sold in the area between the Nera River and the cities of Terni, Spoleto and Norcia. The very high quality black truffles are the most common and they range from the size of a walnut to the size of an orange. The crust is blackish or completely black and irregular (but without any of the roughness that is usually found in black truffle varieties). The interior is dark beige with thin white veins and a brownish red hue. Its aromatic qualities are released when it is heated.

QUICK EASY

Fettuccine con la ricotta

Fettuccine with ricotta

500g egg fettuccine; 350g of sheep ricotta;
½ cup of oil; salt and pepper to taste

Simpler is usually better and the fine local sheep ricotta and fettuccine create a very classy first course.

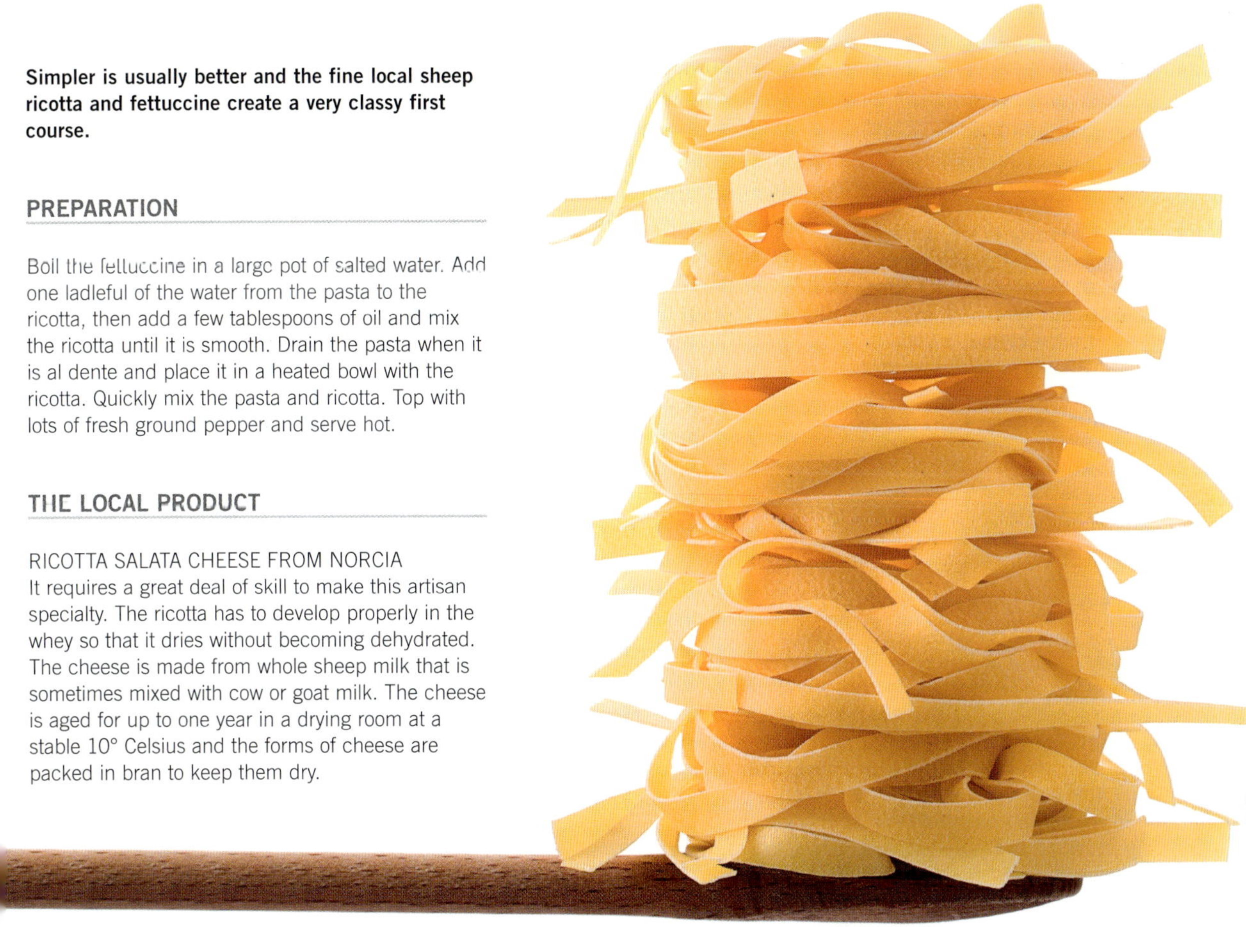

PREPARATION

Boil the fettuccine in a large pot of salted water. Add one ladleful of the water from the pasta to the ricotta, then add a few tablespoons of oil and mix the ricotta until it is smooth. Drain the pasta when it is al dente and place it in a heated bowl with the ricotta. Quickly mix the pasta and ricotta. Top with lots of fresh ground pepper and serve hot.

THE LOCAL PRODUCT

RICOTTA SALATA CHEESE FROM NORCIA
It requires a great deal of skill to make this artisan specialty. The ricotta has to develop properly in the whey so that it dries without becoming dehydrated. The cheese is made from whole sheep milk that is sometimes mixed with cow or goat milk. The cheese is aged for up to one year in a drying room at a stable 10° Celsius and the forms of cheese are packed in bran to keep them dry.

MODERATE

AVERAGE

Risotto alle lenticchie di Castelluccio

Risotto with Castelluccio lentils

200g of rice;
200g of Castelluccio lentils;
1 garlic clove;
200g of tomato chunks (or paste);
½ litre of broth (meat or vegetable broth or bouillon); parsley, olive oil and butter, salt and pepper to taste.

This recipe is a tribute to the star of Umbrian legumes: Castelluccio lentils. The recipe can also be prepared with other kinds of lentils but the flavour might not be the same and you may end up with something that looks more like mashed lentils since many lentil varieties tend to fall apart when they are cooked.

PREPARATION

If you are using Castelluccio lentils, there is no need to soak them beforehand. Parboil the lentils in salted water for around ten minutes. In the meantime dice the garlic and parsley and brown them in oil and butter. When the garlic begins to turn golden in colour, add the tomato sauce and salt and pepper and cook the mixture for 20 minutes. At this point, add the drained lentils and hot broth. Cook for half an hour so that the flavours blend well. Then add the rice and cook it covered over a low flame (the cooking time for the rice depends on the type of rice you are using). Stir occasionally and add more liquid if the mixture becomes too thick. The end result should be creamy but the lentils and rice should not stick together.

THE LOCAL PRODUCT

LENTILS

The study of fossil remains has brought to light that lentils were already being planted in the southern portion of nowadays Syria back in 7000 BC. The lentil quickly spread throughout the Mediterranean to Rome and Greece (Galenus a famous physician from the second century AD spoke of the therapeutic virtues of lentils). They were termed as the 'meat of the poor' due to the fact that they were inexpensive and high in protein. These days in Italy on New Year's Eve, it is customary to give guests a small purse filled with lentils with the wish that they all turn into gold.

Tagliolini alla norcina

Norcina-style tagliolini

400g egg tagliolini egg pasta;
1 truffle (black is generally used but white is also fine);
80g of grated cheese (parmesan or mild pecorino);
50g of butter; extra virgin olive oil, salt and pepper to taste

This is a simple recipe for pasta and truffles that is always a success – truffles transform everything they touch into a true delicacy!

PREPARATION

Prepare the truffle: Use a brush and a damp cloth to clean the truffle. Melt the butter in a pan with 3 or 4 tablespoons of olive oil. Grate the truffle into a warmed bowl, add the grated cheese and pepper to taste. In the meantime, boil the pasta in salted water until it is al dente. Drain the pasta and pour it into the bowl. Add the oil and warm butter and a small ladleful of the water used to cook the pasta. Mix quickly and grate a little fresh truffle over each plate before serving.

THE LOCAL PRODUCT

PECORINO CHEESE FROM NORCIA
This cheese is made from the whole milk of sheep that pasture in Piangrande, Pian Piccolo, Piana di Castelluccio (in the Sibylline Mountains) and the valley of Norcia where water plants and wild herbs grow throughout the year. The fields are filled with watercress and wild celery which provide great forage for the animals all year long. The flavour of the cheese comes from the high quality milk and the rennet, which is made by the shepherds and smoked near a fireplace. The cheese is aged for one year in a cantina at a constant temperature until it is aromatic with a whitish straw colour, a sharp taste and crumbly texture. It is a perfect condiment for topping hearty pasta sauces.

Cosciotto di agnello alla norcina

Norcina-style leg of lamb

TIME CONSUMING AVERAGE

1 leg of lamb (around 1 kilo); 50g prosciutto crudo cut into thick slices; 1 glass of dry white wine; 100g of butter; 300g of potatoes cut into chunks; garlic, parsley, marjoram, salt and pepper to taste.

This dish originates from the area's long history of sheepherding. The recipe does take some time to prepare but it makes a perfect centrepiece dish for an important holiday menu.

PREPARATION

Dice the garlic, parsley and marjoram. Cut the prosciutto into thin strips. Mix the diced mixture and the prosciutto and add salt and pepper. Use the point of a knife or a larder to make deep incisions in the meat and then stuff the ham and diced herbs into the incisions. Brown the lamb in half of the butter over a medium flame. Then cook for around thirty minutes in wine (adding a little at a time). In the meantime brown the potatoes in the rest of the butter and serve together with the leg of lamb.

THE LOCAL PRODUCT

UMBRIAN SALAMI

The art of preserving pork in the Nursine area has been famous since the Imperial Era. The poor mountain areas had long winters that were not well-suited to agriculture and that aided the diffusion of pork farming and sheepherding. With the addition of these activities, the countryside in Lazio and Umbria were exploitable all year long. Sheepherding continued through the Republican and Imperial Roman eras as well as the Pontifical state which followed. Umbria makes many different kinds of salami that reflect the art of fine cuisine in the region. Norcina is an important centre in Umbria for ancient culinary traditions. In fact, master butchers who processed pork were referred to as "Norcini" back in Roman times because they were usually from Norcia or nearby.

Luccio alla perugina

Perugia-style pike

TIME CONSUMING

AVERAGE

Pike grows in Trasimeno Lake which is surrounded by forests that are plentiful in mushrooms. This recipe masterfully blends a creamy mushroom sauce with savoury pike.

1 large pike (around 1 kilo); 100g of porcini mushrooms; 1 glass of white wine; 1 cup of milk; 50g of butter; 1 onion; 1 lemon; salt and pepper to taste

PREPARATION

Line the bottom of a Dutch oven with diced onions and sliced mushrooms. Pour 1 glass of wine and an equal amount of water over the top. Place the fish in the pan and add salt and pepper. Pour the milk in and add several small pats of butter. Cook over a medium flame tor around 15 minutes (occasionally basting the fish with the sauce). Then bake in the oven at 180° Celsius until the fish has turned golden brown and the sauce has thickened. Top with fresh lemon juice before serving.

THE LOCAL PRODUCT

TORGIANO DOC This DOC wine comes from a small group of hills around the Torgiano community where the Chiascio and Tiber rivers meet. The soil, climate and sunshine make these lands particularly well suited for vineyards. The name Torgiano derives from the abbreviation of "Torre di Giano" (or Tower of Janus) which can still be seen in the ancient town even today. Torgiano DOC wine was the first wine in Umbria to receive DOC classification. The range includes white, rosé, red and spumante varieties.

TIME CONSUMING

AVERAGE

DESSERT

Ciaramicola

Ciaramicola Cake

500g flour; a pinch of brewer's yeast; 150g sugar; 2 whole eggs plus two egg whites; 1 bag of candy sprinkles; butter, salt, vanilla, lemon zest, Alchermes and Mistrà liqueur to taste

This classic cake is like a step back in time with a look and a flavour that reminds you of being a kid.

PREPARATION

Prepare a soft dough with 50g of flour, brewer's yeast (dissolved in warm water) and a little salt. Cover the dough and place it in a warm place to rise for 15 minutes. Make a cone from the rest of the flour with an indention at the centre and place the dough in the indention. Then add the beaten whole eggs, sugar, grated lemon zest and vanilla. Knead the dough using a few dashes of Alchermes and Mistrà liqueur to soften the dough. Cover the dough and set it aside for 1 hour. Butter and flour a baking pan and pour in the dough using a wooden spoon to smooth the top. Cover the surface with the beaten egg whites, the sugar and the candy sprinkles. Bake in a pre-heated oven at 160° Celsius until the cake is golden brown. Cool before serving.

THE LOCAL PRODUCT

MONTEFALCO DOC WINE

This DOC wine is made in Montefalco and some of the surrounding towns on the hills south of Perugia. The wine is made from Sagrantino grapes, which are considered by some to be a native variety though there are also a number of other hypotheses. Some believe that the grape variety was imported from Spain while others believe it was imported by the first Franciscans and still others believe it was imported by the Saracens. One certain fact is that these grapes have been growing on Umbria's hills for over a century. The Secco is best with roasts, game, hearty first courses, salami and flavourful cheeses. The Passito is ideal for ending a meal and accompanying baked desserts, pies or Cicerchiata (a local specialty made from honey, almonds and candied fruits), or for sipping in quiet contemplation.

DESSERT

Panpepato
Pepperbread

100g of shelled walnuts, 100g of blanched almonds, 100g of blanched hazelnuts; 100g of citron; 100g of raisins; 150g of dark chocolate; 200g of honey; 2 teaspoons of cinnamon; 1 tablespoon of nutmeg; pepper and white flour to taste

Panpepato is a traditional peppery cake that originated in the countryside around Terni. It was traditionally a Christmas cake but one was always left unopened until Easter or even August 15th for the Feast day of the Assumption of Mary.

PREPARATION

Soak the raisins for around 20 minutes in warm water. Grate the almonds, hazelnuts, walnuts and chocolate and mix them together. Add the citron, two teaspoons of cinnamon powder, one teaspoon of nutmeg powder and lots of ground black pepper. Add the raisins last. Pre-heat the oven to 180°. Line a baking pan with bakery paper. Mix the honey with a little water heat the mixture over a very low flame. When the honey boils, add it to the other ingredients and mix well. Make sure that the chocolate melts completely. Add the flour a little at a time and continue mixing. When the mixture is smooth, use a spoon to break off pieces of dough, form them into balls and place them on a baking pan. Bake for around 10 minutes. After the pepperbread has cooled, remove it from the pan and serve.

THE LOCAL PRODUCT

ORVIETO DOC WINE
This wine is produced between Viterbo and Terni and the historical town of Orvieto is located at the heart of the production area. This is one of the best known Italian wines in the world. The United States alone imports around 2 million bottles per year. The production of this wine represents more than half of the regional total. The Secco variety makes a great aperitif and it pairs well with vegetable dishes, pasta and truffles. The Abboccato and Amabile versions are best with special pairings such as liver, flavourful sharp cheeses, fruit salads, cookies with nuts and traditional desserts.

VALLE D'AOSTA

The magnificent Alpine pastures are filled with the scents of the aromatic herbs used to enhance local cuisine in the Aosta Valley. One of these wild mountain herbs is Artemisia (or wormwood) which is used to make the famous local Génèpy liqueur (similar to absinthe). Another tasty fruit of these mountain pastures is known throughout the world: Fontina cheese. One of the most famous specialties from the Aosta valley, it is also used to make an amazing fondue known as Fonduta. Today it is a DOP certified cheese but it has been around for quite some time. According to a local legend, it was supposedly praised by Pontius Pilate who tasted it while he was with the Roman Legions in Gaul. We find it described in a somewhat veiled yet unmistakeable way in 1267 in a document from the Chatel-Argent di Villeneuve fief. It is even portrayed in castle frescoes in the Aosta Valley with stacks of round Fontina cheese forms being sold at market. There are many references to this classic cheese – a regional symbol loved throughout the world.

The regional cheeses do not stop at Fontina. There are a number of other great varieties with unusual condiments such as Rébléc (a creamy cheese with sugar and cinnamon) and Salignon (ricotta flavoured with oil, garlic and herbs). The salami is also magnificent and it is not always made from pork. Here we find Mocetta, which is made from chamois, goat or beef that is salted and cured. There are also pork specialties including Jambon de Bosses (prosciutto aged for 12 months), Boudin (salami made from sanguinaccio, boiled potatoes, lard and herbs) and the famous seasoned lard of Arnad, which is an ingredient in Boccone Valdostano: a slice of lard on a piece of rye bread topped with Fontina cheese and honey.

The area is famous for its fruit, and especially its apples which are used to make jelly, juice, vinegar and rich desserts. Tegole (a crust of marzipan covered with chocolate) is a local dessert specialty that was borrowed from French culture. Chardé is another almond specialty with honey and fresh citron fruits and Pain des Salasses is a small cake filled with walnuts and chocolate.

WHERE TO FIND VALLE D'AOSTA SPECIALTIES IN ITALY

AOSTA	**OSTERIA DELL'OCA:** Via Edouard Aubert, 15 - Tel.: 0165 231419 **TRATTORIA DEGLI ARTISTI:** Rue Maillet, 5 - Tel.: 0165 40960 **VECCHIA AOSTA:** Piazza Porte Pretoriane, 4 - Tel.: 0165 361186
GENOA	**RISTORANTE PAUL VERLAINE:** Corso Torino, 64/R - Tel.: 010 562166
MILAN	**LA PIERRADE:** Via Abbadesse, 19 - Tel.: 02 6884413
ROME	**TAVERNA LUCIFERO:** Via dei Cappellari, 28 - Tel.: 06 68805536

APPETIZER

Crocchette di fontina

Fontina Croquettes

MODERATE

EASY

50g wheat flour and 50g rice flour (mixed together); 400g of Fontina cheese cut into chunks; 120g of butter; 1 cup of milk; 4 eggs; breadcrumbs, extra virgin olive oil, salt and pepper, ground nutmeg to taste.

These delicious croquettes fill the air with the scent of cheese – truly irresistible for Fontina enthusiasts.

PREPARATION

Mix the flour, milk, 3 eggs, Fontina, butter, salt and nutmeg in a sauce pan. Boil the mixture for 5 minutes stirring constantly. Then pour the mixture into a bowl and allow it to cool. Use the mixture to form small croquettes. Dip each croquette in beaten egg and breadcrumbs and deep fry. Serve hot.

THE LOCAL PRODUCT

FONTINA CHEESE

The name Fontina comes from the mountain town of Font in the Municipality of Quart. The cheese is produced exclusively in the Aosta Valley and the first references to it date back to the year 1200. However, the name Fontina appears for the first time in the accounting records of a charitable institution named Gran San Bernardo in 1717. The cheese is mild and delicious with an elastic and soft consistency that melts in the mouth. Fontina is made with whole milk and natural flavours – nothing is added and nothing is removed. The milk is not skimmed or pasteurized so the nutritional and organoleptic qualities remain intact.

MODERATE

EASY

Polenta valdostana

Aosta Valley Polenta

500g of polenta (cooked, poured into a pan to cool and sliced); 8 slices of Fontina cheese; 300g tomato sauce; extra virgin olive oil, salt and pepper to taste

In the Aosta Valley polenta is eaten on a daily basis all year long. There are an infinite variety of ways to prepare it ranging from elaborate to simple. The common thread is the creamy flavourful Fontina cheese topping. This easy basic recipe is one example.

PREPARATION

Lay the polenta slices in a pan and bake at 220° Celsius until they are well toasted. In the meantime prepare a simple sauce with tomato sauce, olive oil, salt and pepper. After removing the polenta from the oven, top each slice of polenta with a slice of Fontina cheese and a spoonful of sauce. Toast under the grill for a couple of minutes and serve hot.

THE LOCAL PRODUCT

VALLE D'AOSTA DOC WINE

This is the only large Protected Designation of Origin (DOC) that unites all of the winemaking areas throughout the region, which is divided into seven wine subzones. The grapes are cultivated in towns along the Dora Baltea River at around 800 to 1200 metres above sea level. Here the cool winter climate and hot dry summers are perfect for the grapes which are made into several different varieties of wine.

Zuppa di cavolo verza

Savoy cabbage soup

TIME CONSUMING

EASY

1 Savoy cabbage (800g cleaned cabbage); 120g of Fontina or Fromadzo cheese; 80g grated parmesan; 50g melted butter; 8 slices of bread without the crust; salt to taste.

This creamy dense soup is a classic mountain specialty and it is a perfect choice for cold winter evenings.

PREPARATION

Parboil the cabbage leaves in salted water then drain it and cut it into thin strips. Boil the strips in just ½ litre of water and once they have finished cooking, drain the cabbage and set the broth aside. Line the bottom of a large casserole dish with bread slices and cover it with a layer of cabbage and a layer of Fontina cheese. Top with parmesan and a ladleful of broth then add another topping of parmesan and melted butter and bake at 140° for about 45 minutes.

THE LOCAL PRODUCT

FROMADZO VALLEY

The first documented references of Fromadzo cheese in the Aosta Valley are contained in a note of the "Summa Lacticiniorum" by Pantaleone da Confienza. Since antiquity the local people have been making this cheese as an alternative to Fontina. The milk left over from the production of Fontina was used to make Fromadzo which was longer lasting and served as a good protein source. Pantaleone mentions a medium-sized form of cheese with a thick crust, a compact grain and a dense texture - and that is how it is traditionally made in the Aosta Valley. Other references from the sixteen hundreds mention a cheese that is only identified as "fromage commun" or "fromage ordinaire" (common or ordinary cheese).

TIME CONSUMING

AVERAGE

Carbonada

Carbonada Beef Stew

700g beef cut into three thick slices; 80g butter; 1 onion; 4 glasses of white wine and 4 glasses of red wine; 2 garlic cloves; rosemary, sage, bay leaves, cloves, juniper berries and salt to taste.

The Aosta valley produces fine beef and this recipe makes the most of the local meat with herbs and fragrant juniper. For this recipe it is important to use very fresh beef.

PREPARATION

Place the slices of meat in a large container with a tight seal. Top the meat with herbs, garlic and salt and then refrigerate the mixture for at least 2 days. When you are ready to cook the meat, dice an onion very finely and brown it in a little butter until it falls apart. Add the red and white wine, a little salt and cook over a low flame. After a few minutes, add the cloves and juniper berries. In the meantime cut the meat into small chunks and brown it in a non-stick pan in a little butter until it is golden brown on both sides. As the meat turns golden place it in the pan with the sauce and cook it for another 10 minutes. If the sauce is not thick enough, mix two tablespoons of sauce with one tablespoon of flour, pour the mixture in and cook for another few minutes until the sauce thickens.

THE LOCAL PRODUCT

LARD D'ARNAND

The first documents that refer to fatback cured in brine with herbs and spices in the Aosta Valley date back to a manuscript from 1570 in reference to the cafeteria of the Monastery of Santo Orso and the distribution of food products to the poor. In 1763, the first inventory of the castle of Arnad lists that the castle had four 'doils' (wooden containers used to season and preserve the lard). The first references regarding prices of the product date back to the 18th century. Another later reference describes a tavern in Aosta where the list of foods on a large tablet includes Lard Friand (choice lard). Today this local tradition still continues and many families raise a couple of pigs each year to sell the lard at the town festival on the last Sunday in August.

SECOND COURSES

Fonduta

Fondue

TIME CONSUMING

EASY

400g Fontina cheese cut into chunks; 4 egg yolks; 30g butter; 50g of cream; 6 slices Italian bread cut into chunks and fried; milk to taste.

This is the region's most popular specialty even though the recipe is relatively modern. Fonduta was invented by the personal chef of the Count of Cavour, but it was based on the older French recipe fondue. It is a hearty winter dish and it is also great for topping rice or toasted bread. It is even better with white truffle slivers grated on top.

PREPARATION

Soak the cheese in milk for at least 8 hours. Drain off most of the milk before cooking. Use a double boiler to cook the cheese, cream and butter (stirring constantly) until they melt but make sure the mixture does not boil. Add the egg yolks and mix well. Serve directly from the double boiler so that the fondue stays nice and hot. Place fried bread into each bowl and top it with a few ladlefuls of the sauce and fresh ground black pepper.

THE LOCAL PRODUCT

FONTINA D'ALPEGGIO CHEESE

This cheese was already around during medieval times (it is described in detail in the famous Summa Lacticinorum). The milk used to make this cheese comes from a breed of cows that are only raised here: the Pezzata Valdostana. The cows are pastured in the high mountains where they feed on fragrant grasses. The very best Fontina comes from Valtournanche, where two alpine farms have the honour of having invented it: Fontin in Quart and Fontinaz in St. Marcel. The cheese is made from fresh milk (milked no more than two hours before the cheese is made). After a rather laborious preparation it is aged in forms that range from eight to eighteen kilos. It gives the local specialties their unmistakeable flavour and it triumphs in "fonduta".

Fricandò dama bianca

Fricandò dama bianca veal

500g veal chunks; 1 leek; 1 glass of white wine; 50g of melted butter; flour and salt to taste.

This veal specialty derives from French cuisine and Fricandeau was mentioned by Rabelais in his books about the giant Pantagruel and his adventures in food. This dish is a traditional specialty served on August 5th throughout the region for the Our Lady of the Snow feast day. The dish owes its name to this holiday - 'Dama Bianca' means Lady in White.

PREPARATION

Cut the leek into thin slices and brown it in butter over a low flame in a large pan. Add the meat and brown it on all sides. Then salt the meat and add one glass of white wine. Cover the pan and cook for around 40 minutes. In a cup, mix two tablespoons of flour with a few spoonfuls of the drippings. Pour the mixture back into the pan and cook for another 3 minutes (stirring constantly).

THE LOCAL PRODUCT

JAMBON DE BOSSES HAM

The pork is salt cured and seasoned with ground pepper, sage, rosemary, garlic, juniper, thyme and bay for around twenty days. During that time it is massaged to help eliminate any excess liquids. Then it is dried and aged. Before curing, the tip of the femur and the meat surfaces are rubbed with lots of black ground pepper. When it is cut, the meat is wine red with a smooth texture. The lard is firm and shiny with a pinkish tinge towards the exterior. It has a delicate flavour that is slightly savoury but mild with an aromatic hint and a slightly untamed taste. The most ancient references to this product date back to 1397 and mention that it existed in the Saint-Rhémy-en-Bosses area indicated as "tybias porci".

VENETO

The culinary traditions of Veneto are like a bridge between two worlds that are both rich in characteristic specialties. The sea front area is tied to the history of Venice and seafood while the large inland area has good farmland with large plains, ample water and even pastures and mountains. These lands produce rice and polenta that are important staples in Veneto (the local varieties are excellent: Marano Vicentino corn and Vialone Nano rice).

The interior lands provide a host of fine vegetables to flavour great recipes: Lamon beans, Trevigiano radicchio (as well as a number of other wonderful varieties) and asparagus (including the ever-popular white asparagus). As we climb higher we find dairy farms that make fine cheeses such as Asiago and Piave. There are also excellent meats including the local specialty Bondiola Vicentina (similar to cotechino but made from prime cuts of meat), which pairs well with polenta, beans and sauerkraut, Soppressa and Luganega Trevignana.

There is also an ample choice of seafood specialties. Alongside fish, molluscs and crustaceans from the sea, we find an active local fish farming industry in the lagoons which provide a tasty selection of eel, mussels and sea bass. Fresh water fish are also plentiful in the many rivers and Garda Lake.

The local contact with the sea led to more than just seafood specialties. Contact with the cultures of the east introduced the fragrances and flavours of the orient into the cuisine of Veneto. A couple of examples include Sardines in Saor Sauce, which are flavoured with raisins and spices or Pane Arabo di Castelfranco bread which is very similar to falafel bread). The dessert that best reflects this influence is Pinza, which is traditionally served on the Epiphany. It combines local flavours like polenta, squash and apples with flavours that speak of the southern Mediterranean such as citron, raisins and dried figs.

WHERE TO FIND VENETO SPECIALTIES IN ITALY

MILAN	**LA TANA DEL LUPO:** Viale Vittorio Veneto, 30 - Tel.: 02 6599006 **RISTORANTE BELL'ARIA:** Via Meda, 43 - Tel.: 02 89501448 **RISTORANTE SANTINI:** Via San Marco, 3 - Tel.: 02 6555587
ROME	**OMBRE E CICHETI:** Via del Lago Terrione, 18 - Tel.: 06 633280
TURIN	**CIACOLON CA' VENETA:** Viale XXV Aprile, 11 - Tel.: 011 6610911
VENICE	**CANTINA DO SPADE:** Calle delle Do Spade, 19 - Tel.: 041 5210583 **OSTERIA AL PORTEGO:** Calle della Malvasia - Tel.: 041 5229038 **OSTARIA DA MARIANO:** Via Cecchini, 1 - Mestre - Tel.: 041 615765

APPETIZER

Sardelle in saor

Sardines in Saor sauce

600g cleaned anchovies; 2 onions; 50g pine nuts; 50g raisins (soaked in warm water); flour, vinegar, extra virgin olive oil and salt to taste.

MODERATE

AVERAGE

These marinated sardines are a popular specialty all along the coast of Veneto. The addition of pine nuts and raisins reflects the influence of contact with peoples of the East. Pine nuts and raisins are not required but they are very good.

PREPARATION

Wash the sardines and drain well. Dip each sardine in flour and then deep fry until it is golden brown on both sides. Lay the fish on a paper towel to absorb any excess oil and top with salt. Use another pan and different oil to brown a sliced onion. As soon as the onion turns golden in colour, add the vinegar and cook for a few minutes. Place the sardines in a container and cover each layer of fish with a little bit of the onion sauce and the pine nuts and raisins. Top with more vinegar so that the liquid completely covers the sardines. Close the container and allow it to marinate in a cool place for 24-48 hours before serving.

THE LOCAL PRODUCT

CORTI BENEDETTINE DEL PADOVANO WINE

"Corti Benedettine del Padovano" wine received DOC recognition in June 2004. The production area runs from the southeast end of the Padua province to the southern end of the Venice province. It is grown in an area that was inhabited by monks from the Benedictine Abbey of Santa Giustina in Padua for 700 years (from the 12th century to the 19th century). Corti Benedettine was the administrative, economic and social heart of the lands and it managed the grounds and developed the land by reclaiming the soil, banking the rivers, constructing rural buildings and cultivating the land under the guidance of the monks. Grapes have been cultivated here since Roman times and there are many vineyards throughout the area. The wine produced in the Corti cantinas became one of the major trading commodities with the cities of Padua and Venice. Venice then sold the wine throughout the ports in the Mediterranean.

TIME CONSUMING

EASY

Panada

400g dry hard-grain bread; 350g stew meat; 1 onion; 1 carrot and 1 stalk of celery; 2 ripe cherry tomatoes; 1 level teaspoon of cinnamon; 80g of grated parmesan cheese; extra virgin olive oil and salt to taste

Panada is a traditional bread stew specialty. Recipes like this made from dry bread were common in the past when people took care to not waste anything. This dish turns stale bread into a rich specialty with chopped meat and vegetables.

PREPARATION

Boil the meat with diced onion, carrot, celery and cherry tomatoes. Cook for about half an hour (add salt after 15 minutes). In the meantime, slice the bread and lay it on the bottom of a ceramic baking dish, cover it with broth and allow the bread time to absorb all the liquid. Then add more broth. Sprinkle with cinnamon and half of the cheese and bake at 190° Celsius for around 40 minutes. Top with a little olive oil and the rest of the cheese, and let it cool for 2 minutes before serving.

THE LOCAL PRODUCT

VALPOLICELLA WINE
This DOC wine is made in a group of valleys at the foot of the Monti Lessini mountains. The area includes 19 municipalities in northern Verona. The vineyards have a continental climate that makes the wine full-bodied with an intense colour. A favourite of Virgil, it was perfected over the centuries and became increasingly popular. The red is a perfect table wine and it is available in several varieties: the standard version is perfect for first courses with hearty toppings, grilled meats, roast chicken, salami and flavourful cheeses that are not too intense. Amarone is best with roasts or sharp flavourful cheeses while the Recioto is a dessert wine or after dinner wine to be accompanied by fruit pies, almond cakes and biscotti.

TIME CONSUMING

AVERAGE

FIRST COURSES

Risi e bisi

Rice and peas

300g rice; 300g peas (the peas and the hulls); ½ litre of vegetable broth; 30g butter; 1 diced onion; 80g grated parmesan; diced parsley, extra virgin olive oil and salt to taste

This unusual recipe is a very popular regional dish and a true delight.

PREPARATION

Wash the pea hulls and boil them in salted water for around 1 hour. Use a spoon to scrape the green creamy substance from inside the hulls. Brown the diced onion in oil. Then add a little water, the peas and a little broth and simmer for a few minutes. Continue adding the broth (mixed with the green cream from the pea hulls) and boil. When the mixture boils add the rice and cook for around 15 minutes (stirring constantly). Top with butter, cheese and parsley before serving.

THE LOCAL PRODUCT

VIALONE RICE

The Persians discovered Vialone rice in the 5th century BC. From there it spread to Syria and Egypt and the therapeutic qualities of rice water even interested Greek and Roman physicians. In Europe it was only cultivated by the Moors in Iberia and Portugal in the 1400s. Two centuries earlier the vice county of Milan attempted to produce rice, but the project was abandoned due to the extensive problems with malaria. In Italy, rice began to take root in 1486. In the 16th century the production areas in Lombardy and Piedmont extended greatly. The variety of Vialone Nano rice created by the Stazione Sperimentale di Risicoltura in Vercelli was made by crossing the Nano variety with the Vialone variety which has been cultivated since 1937 and was introduced into the province of Verona in 1945.

QUICK

EASY

Fegato alla veneziana

Venetian-style liver

400g sliced veal liver; 500g finely sliced onions;
30g butter; grated parsley;
extra virgin olive oil, salt and pepper to taste

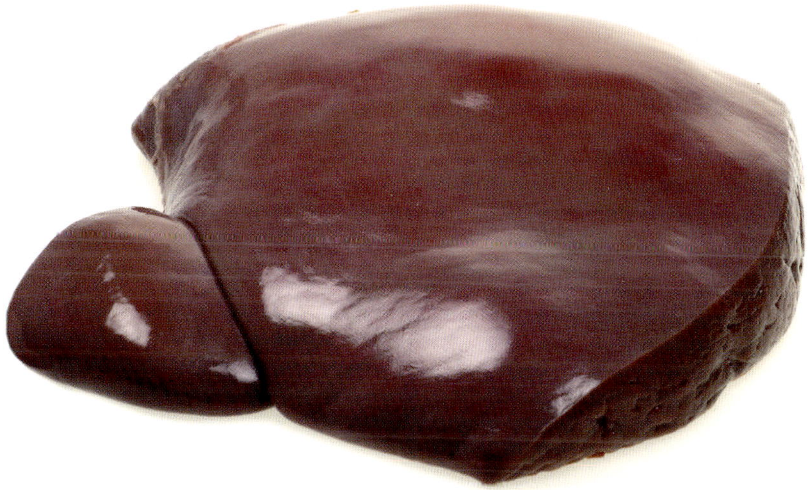

This liver and onion recipe is used throughout Italy – it is an absolutely perfect balance between simplicity and flavour.

PREPARATION

Melt the butter in a pan with the oil and brown the onions. Then add a cup of warm water and cook for 10 minutes. Add the liver slices and cook over a high flame for 5 minutes. Serve the liver with the onion sauce.

THE LOCAL PRODUCT

OLIVE OIL FROM VENETO

Olives were introduced into the Veneto region by the Roman colonies, but the first references date back to the 9th century. Olive cultivation has had moments of great success and expansion and moments of crisis due to economic and climatic reasons. It expanded greatly after World War I thanks to the financial support of local institutions. The first reference to the product dates back to 1500 while the quality of olive oil from Veneto and its organoleptic qualities are described in a written work from the past century.

SECOND COURSES

Stoccafisso alla vicentina

Vicenza-style Stockfish

700g stockfish (soaked, skinned, deboned and opened up);
200g of sliced onions; 4 diced anchovy fillets; 1 garlic clove;
1 cup of milk; 40g of flour; 40g of grated parmesan;
diced parsley, extra virgin olive oil and salt and pepper to taste

This is an absolute classic in Veneto. This stockfish recipe is very similar to the Treviso version, except for the savoury addition of the anchovy paste and garlic. The preparation is really very different and much more elaborate. This tasty specialty is for great chefs.

PREPARATION

Brown the garlic, onion and parsley in oil. Add the anchovies after a couple of minutes and cook into a sauce. Open the fish up and spread the sauce inside then top the sauce with flour, cheese, salt and pepper. Close the fish back up and dip it in flour and then grated cheese. Cut the fish into fillets and place them in a broad low pan (ceramic if possible). Top with the milk and diced garlic and parsley and cook over a very low flame for 3 hours.

THE LOCAL PRODUCT

SOAVE WINE

The production area for this wine is located in the eastern part of a hilly arch in the province of Verona where it grows on volcanic lands composed of tuff stone, clay and limestone. Soave is the heart of the production area and the name most likely derives from the time of the Longobard invasion when the Swabians were also referred to as "Suavi". Soave DOC wine is one of the oldest types of Italian wines and it was mentioned by Cassiodorus, Dante and even Gabriele D'Annunzio. The soave is ideal for delicate appetizers, soups, pasta and rice dishes with fresh light toppings, egg dishes, seafood specialties and white meats The spumante is great with fruit pies, and oven baked desserts.

TIME CONSUMING

DIFFICULT

MODERATE

EASY

Fagioli in salsa

Beans in Sauce

1 kilo of fresh beans (or 500g of dried beans soaked for 12 hours); 2 garlic cloves; 8 ground anchovy fillets; vinegar, extra virgin olive oil and salt to taste.

The Veneto region has excellent beans and they are a common ingredient in local recipes. This 'solo' version is absolutely delectable.

PREPARATION

Boil the beans in salted water and drain them when they ıre soft but not mushy. Separately brown the crushed garlic clove (remove it from the oil when it is golden in colour). Then add the anchovies and mix for a couple of minutes over a medium flame before adding ½ cup of vinegar. Continue cooking until the sauce thickens then pour the hot anchovy sauce over the beans, mix well nd serve.

THE LOCAL PRODUCT

LAMON BEANS

The unique qualities of Lamon Beans come from the special climatic conditions in the area which are perfect for legumes. The beans are still produced with the traditional methods: they are carefully selected and patiently processed. Lamon beans are traditionally planted on May third on Day of the Holy Cross and they are harvested from the second half of August to the end of September. There are four main varieties: Spagnolo, Calonega, Canalino and Spagnolit. The Spagnolo variety has an oval shape and a fine skin. The Spagnolit has a thicker round shape, a more delicate flavour and especially tender skin. The Calonega variety is cultivated both for its high yield and excellent qualities and the Canalino has soft red veining.

Alphabetical index of the recipes

Alphabetical index of the recipes

Photo References

FOTOLIA.COM - Schiaffoni Tricolore © Fotograv A. Gravante Cover

FOTOLIA.COM - parsley tied isolated © Diana Taliun Pg. 1
FOTOLIA.COM - wine bottle and young grape vine © fox17 8
FOTOLIA.COM - alive squid seafood isolated on white © lunamarina 9
FOTOLIA.COM - oro giallo © MAMODA 9
FOTOLIA.COM - Hartkäse zum Reiben © Doris Heinrichs 10
FOTOLIA.COM - Spaghetti alla chitarra, pasta fresca fatta a mano © Stefano Neri 10
FOTOLIA.COM - minestrone2 © roby67foto 11
FOTOLIA.COM - antipasto di mare © Alexandra 12
FOTOLIA.COM - Roast turkey on a board © Paul Cowan 13
FOTOLIA.COM - Roher Thunfisch © ExQuisine 14
FOTOLIA.COM - ricotta with basil - ricotta con basilico © Marco Mayer 18
FOTOLIA.COM - torta salata di farro farcita con ortaggi di primavera © spinetta 18
FOTOLIA.COM - lagane aux pois chiches - lagane with chickpeas © S.E. Shooting 19
FOTOLIA.COM - piece of meat on a fork isolated on white background © Bernd Jürgens 20
FOTOLIA.COM - Cipolle gialle © Roberto Fasoli 20
FOTOLIA.COM - wine bottle © Albo 20
FOTOLIA.COM - Seppie in umido © MarcoBagnoli Elflaco 21
FOTOLIA.COM - verde e rosso © Guagui 22
FOTOLIA.COM - Miel © Frog 974 23
FOTOLIA.COM - vanilla flowered © amridesign 23
FOTOLIA.COM - carrot soup-zuppa di carote © Marco Mayer 26
FOTOLIA.COM - red onion © matka_Wariatka 26
FOTOLIA.COM - mixed legumes © Tinka 27
FOTOLIA.COM - lasagne sheets © Jiri Hera 28
FOTOLIA.COM - Uova sode © Comugnero Silvana 28
FOTOLIA.COM - Ravioli ripieni © Alessio Cola 29
FOTOLIA.COM - Food collection isolated on white background © Elena Schweitzer 29
FOTOLIA.COM - three fresh mandarin close-up isolated on a white background © bota horatiu 30
FOTOLIA.COM - Herbs and spices collection © photka 30
FOTOLIA.COM - Noce © fabiomax 31
FOTOLIA.COM - Uva passa © Comugnero Silvana 31
FOTOLIA.COM - mozzarella © Giuseppe Porzani 34
FOTOLIA.COM - Pizza Margherita con mozzarella di bufala © Fotograv A. Gravante 35
FOTOLIA.COM - Riso e Funghi Porcini © claudio 36
FOTOLIA.COM - red wine pouring down from a wine bottle © Ljupco Smokovski 37
FOTOLIA.COM - Pasta al forno. Italian food. © Mi.Ti. 37
FOTOLIA.COM - pezzo di carne per arrosto di vitello © Giuseppe Porzani 38
FOTOLIA.COM - pasticcini © Giuseppe Porzani 39
FOTOLIA.COM - Pastiera napoletana - Cucina partenopea © Comugnero Silvana 40
FOTOLIA.COM - Struffoli napoletani © SCPixBit 41
FOTOLIA.COM - White wine © Igor Dutina 41
FOTOLIA.COM - Bietola da coste sullo sfondo bianco © Vasileva 44
FOTOLIA.COM - Blardons © claireliz 44
FOTOLIA.COM - Brodo © ivanozinelli 45
FOTOLIA.COM - Lasagna © Joe Gough 46
FOTOLIA.COM - tagliatelle and other ingredients © mark huls 47
FOTOLIA.COM - yellow pumpkin vegetable with green leaves © Yasonya 48
FOTOLIA.COM - collection of homemade italian pasta © Marco Mayer 48
FOTOLIA.COM - Baccalà © Lorenzo Buttitta 49
FOTOLIA.COM - Food collection isolated on white background © Elena Schweitzer 49
FOTOLIA.COM - Cotechino sul tagliere © Studio Gi 50
FOTOLIA.COM - Herbs and spices collection © photka 50
FOTOLIA.COM - escalope de veau © Magalice 51
FOTOLIA.COM - Boccetta di aceto © Roberto Fasoli 51
FOTOLIA.COM - Enogastronomia © alicedurigatto 54
FOTOLIA.COM - Borlotti 4 09 © Orlando Bellini 55
FOTOLIA.COM - preparing sauerkraut © Hallgerd 55
Burrida - Foto Marco Scataglini 55
FOTOLIA.COM - spinach leaves © arnowssr 56
FOTOLIA.COM - bacalao © nito 57
FOTOLIA.COM - Herbs and spices collection © photka 57
FOTOLIA.COM - Turnip isolated over white © Stefano Tiraboschi 58
FOTOLIA.COM - decanter con bicchiere di vino © scatto 58
FOTOLIA.COM - calice di vino © vagabondo 59
FOTOLIA.COM - Gubana - Dolce tipico delle Valli del Natisone - Friuli © Comugnero Silvana 59
FOTOLIA.COM - Herbs and spices collection © photka 62
FOTOLIA.COM - artichoke © rimglow 62
FOTOLIA.COM - Bucatini © Marzia Giacobbe 63
FOTOLIA.COM - ilmax72 A0872 © www.ilmax72.com 64
FOTOLIA.COM - pecorino stagionato nel fieno © spinetta 64
FOTOLIA.COM - Pasta © Marzia Giacobbe 65
FOTOLIA.COM - silhouette of summer garden bbq isolated against f © LockStockBob 66
FOTOLIA.COM - Saltimbocca alla romana © petrabarz 67
FOTOLIA.COM - verdura su piatto con posate su sfondo bianco © Fabrizio Vinti 68
FOTOLIA.COM - Maritozzo con la panna © Marzia Giacobbe 69
FOTOLIA.COM - Delicious pine nuts © Lasse Kristensen 69
FOTOLIA.COM - tuna © Aaron Amat 72
FOTOLIA.COM - Ramo d'ulivo © francovolpato 72
FOTOLIA.COM - Torta pasqualina © spinetta 73
FOTOLIA.COM - salsa di noci © Alexandra 74
FOTOLIA.COM - Löffel mit frischer Ravioli © Angela Shirinov 74
FOTOLIA.COM - pasta al pesto © Henry Bonn 75
FOTOLIA.COM - Funghi Porcini secchi © Comugnero Silvana Pg. 76
FOTOLIA.COM - Cauliflower © Tomboy2290 77
FOTOLIA.COM - Seppie in zimino - Secondi di pesce Toscana © Comugnero Silvana 78
FOTOLIA.COM - Fruits confits © bricef 79
FOTOLIA.COM - White Wine © rimglow 79
FOTOLIA.COM - Isolated bunch of wheat © Rido 79
FOTOLIA.COM - minced beef © claireliz 82
FOTOLIA.COM - Farina doppio zero © Comugnero Silvana 82
FOTOLIA.COM - Pizzoccheri della Valtellina © Comugnero Silvana 83
FOTOLIA.COM - Maize flour in the bag - gluten free, isolated © Nika Novak 84
FOTOLIA.COM - Risotto alla zucca. risotto with pumpkin © Lorenzo Galluzzi 85
FOTOLIA.COM - mix di carne con sfondo bianco © double click 86
FOTOLIA.COM - Celery root © Leonid Nyshko 86
FOTOLIA.COM - cotoletta con osso © Giuseppe Porzani 87
FOTOLIA.COM - ossobuco,geschmorte kalbshaxe,klassische italienisch © Lucky Dragon 88
FOTOLIA.COM - Almond © kaanates 89
FOTOLIA.COM - Torta di mandorle sbrisolona - Dolci della cucina lombarda © Comugnero Silvana 89
FOTOLIA.COM - Olive ascolane © Fabio Galli © bit24 92
FOTOLIA.COM - tiger shrimps isolated on white © bit24 93
FOTOLIA.COM - Fogli di pasta sfoglia per lasagne © Sergiogen 94
FOTOLIA.COM - cut beef on white background © Andre 94
FOTOLIA.COM - Baccalà © francovolpato 95
FOTOLIA.COM - Patata a fette © Franco Deriu 95
FOTOLIA.COM - Red Mullet (Rotbarbe) © Picturefoods.com 96
FOTOLIA.COM - dried figs © ostromec 97
FOTOLIA.COM - chocolate&coffee_1 © carlos Restrepo 97
FOTOLIA.COM - riso italiano su cucchiaio di legno © Giuseppe Porzani 97
FOTOLIA.COM - caciocavallo typical italian cheese © Marco Mayer 100
FOTOLIA.COM - Cavatelli Pugliesi © Lorenzo Buttitta 101
FOTOLIA.COM - Vino 49 © Luis Carlos Jiménez 101
FOTOLIA.COM - Squid © artemisphoto 102
FOTOLIA.COM - pouring white wine © Roman Sigaev 102
FOTOLIA.COM - Capperi - Capparis spinosa © Comugnero Silvana 102
FOTOLIA.COM - semi di finocchio © spinetta 103
FOTOLIA.COM - pork meat sausages © nito 103
FOTOLIA.COM - Bell peppers: red, green, yellow in raw. © Kate Bialasiewicz 104
FOTOLIA.COM - pasta sfoglia © shooterg03 105
FOTOLIA.COM - broken egg on white © Elenathewise 105
FOTOLIA.COM - white truffle © luca manieri 108
FOTOLIA.COM - Frische Gnocchi © Carmen Steiner 108
FOTOLIA.COM - glass red wine © Alexandr Shebanov 109
FOTOLIA.COM - riso © DAV 110
FOTOLIA.COM - Bollito misto - Secondi di carne del Veneto © Comugnero Silvana5 111
FOTOLIA.COM - The best crop of this year © valeriy555 112
FOTOLIA.COM - manzo © Lsantilli 112
FOTOLIA.COM - Bagna Cauda , italian warm dip © uckyo 113
FOTOLIA.COM - Herbs and spices collection © photka 113
FOTOLIA.COM - baci di dama © Giuseppe Porzani 114
FOTOLIA.COM - milk © Okea 115
FOTOLIA.COM - Bonet budino tipico © spinetta 115
FOTOLIA.COM - CALZONE MIT BEILAGEN © Herby (Herbert) Me 118
FOTOLIA.COM - Black olives. © Angel Simon 118
FOTOLIA.COM - homemade orecchiette typical italian pasta © Marco Mayer 119
FOTOLIA.COM - broccoli © motorlka 119
FOTOLIA.COM - Chili peppers © Pixis 119
Pancotto - Foto Marco Scataglini 120
FOTOLIA.COM - Finocchietto 01 04 10 © Orlando Bellini 121
FOTOLIA.COM - olive oil © volff 121
FOTOLIA.COM - Patate a fette © Franco Deriu 121
FOTOLIA.COM - Pile of brown long rice isolated over white © slavson 122
FOTOLIA.COM - The best crop of this year © valeriy555 122
FOTOLIA.COM - Mussel © Maceo 122
FOTOLIA.COM - triglia © Lsantilli 123
FOTOLIA.COM - Rosemary © fotogal 123
FOTOLIA.COM - Oil and vinegar © Nikola Bilic 124
FOTOLIA.COM - mint © Eldin Muratovic 124
FOTOLIA.COM - Cipolle in agrodolce - Antipasti Lombardia © Comugnero Silvana 124
FOTOLIA.COM - Lemon © volff 125
FOTOLIA.COM - russian traditional pancakes pile on plate © DLeonis 125
FOTOLIA.COM - Pane Carasau fatto in casa © Orlando Bellini 128
FOTOLIA.COM - pecorino © spinetta 128
FOTOLIA.COM - bowl with san marzano tomatoes, basil and spoon © Marco Mayer 128
FOTOLIA.COM - coste cesto © antimage 129
Malloreddus - Foto Marco Scataglini 130
FOTOLIA.COM - la spaghettata © double click 131
FOTOLIA.COM - walnut © AGphotographer 132
FOTOLIA.COM - Pinoli © Comugnero Silvana 132
FOTOLIA.COM - lardo © effe45 133
FOTOLIA.COM - cerises Brésil, Eugenia brasiliensis, fond blanc © Unclesam 133
FOTOLIA.COM - pesci © fophoto 134
FOTOLIA.COM - traditional sardinian dessert "seadas" with honey © nextyle 135
FOTOLIA.COM - miele © Alexandra 135
FOTOLIA.COM - Pila di formaggio © DAN 138
FOTOLIA.COM - Arancini di Riso © Orlando Bellini 138
FOTOLIA.COM - Italian Pasta with tomatoes and basil © Maksim Shebeko Pg. 139
FOTOLIA.COM - ricotta © antimage 139
FOTOLIA.COM - Eggplants on a white studio background © eAlisa 139
FOTOLIA.COM - Sardine © Fotograv A. Gravante 140
FOTOLIA.COM - pasta italiana © Giuseppe Porzani 140
FOTOLIA.COM - Three pears in a row over white background © Sandra van der Steen 141
FOTOLIA.COM - Filetto di baccala al forno - Secondi di pesce del Veneto © Comugnero Silvana 141
FOTOLIA.COM - uovo © Veruska1969 142
FOTOLIA.COM - Carpaccio di vitellone © Studio Gi 142
FOTOLIA.COM - Tomaten & Basilikum © Andrea Wilhelm 143
FOTOLIA.COM - melanzanas © imagestalk 143
FOTOLIA.COM - cannoli sicily dessert © Marco Mayer 144
FOTOLIA.COM - Cassate © Marzia Giacobbe 145
FOTOLIA.COM - Crostino rustico al paté di fegato © MarcoBagnoli Elflaco 148
FOTOLIA.COM - salt & pepper shaker © rimglow 148
FOTOLIA.COM - pane toscano © spinetta 148
FOTOLIA.COM - Acquacotta casentinese - Cucina della toscana © Comugnero Silvana 149
FOTOLIA.COM - Herbs and spices collection © photka 149
FOTOLIA.COM - Puro aceita de Oliva. © gosphotodesign 150
FOTOLIA.COM - Pappa al pomodoro - Primi Toscana © Comugnero Silvana 150
FOTOLIA.COM - bietole © spinetta 151
FOTOLIA.COM - fagioli © Giuseppe Porzani 151
FOTOLIA.COM - polpo 2 © Giuseppe Porzani 152
FOTOLIA.COM - Triglie alla livornese - Secondi di pesce della Toscana © Comugnero Silvana 153
FOTOLIA.COM - Sugo Freschissimo © Orlando Bellini 154
FOTOLIA.COM - Plate of beans © Lorenzo Buttitta © Lorenzo Buttitta 154
FOTOLIA.COM - pinoli © Alexandra 155
FOTOLIA.COM - castagna © FEG 155
FOTOLIA.COM - pane tipico alto adige © Giuseppe Porzani 158
FOTOLIA.COM - formaggio grana con coltello © Marco Mayer 158
FOTOLIA.COM - Knodel in Brodo © MarcoBagnoli Elflaco 158
FOTOLIA.COM - speck © antimage 159
FOTOLIA.COM - slice potato on white background © Andre 159
FOTOLIA.COM - Orzo perlato - Hordeum vulgare © Comugnero Silvana 159
FOTOLIA.COM - viande de boeuf découpée pour bourguignon © Maurice Metzger 160
FOTOLIA.COM - Lemon zest on a zester. Shallow depth of field © robynmac 160
FOTOLIA.COM - Vino e uva © Studio Gi 160
FOTOLIA.COM - Herbs and spices collection © photka 161
FOTOLIA.COM - cabbage © ivan kmit 161
FOTOLIA.COM - filetto al pepe verde © Lsantilli. 161
FOTOLIA.COM - Sgonfiotti alla frutta - Susse gebackene krapfen - Dolci T A A © Comugnero Silvana 162
FOTOLIA.COM - Blueberry isolated on white background © Alessio Cola 162
FOTOLIA.COM - Apfelstrudel (apple pie) © Catalin Petolea 163
FOTOLIA.COM - mele rosse © Alexandra 163
FOTOLIA.COM - Truffe en coupe © lamax 166
FOTOLIA.COM - ricotta cheese © elmapo 167
FOTOLIA.COM - Pila di tagliatelle © DAN 167
FOTOLIA.COM - Burlap sack with lentils spilling out over a white background © Rafa Irusta 168
FOTOLIA.COM - olio d'oliva extravergine © piumadaquila.com 168
FOTOLIA.COM - Trüffel © Christoph Hähnel 169
FOTOLIA.COM - Fettuccine all'uovo © Comugnero Silvana 169
FOTOLIA.COM - Raw Lamb Shanks © Tomboy2290 170
FOTOLIA.COM - Cut potato isolated on white background. © Borys Shevchuk 170
FOTOLIA.COM - predatory fish on the white © Yasonya 171
FOTOLIA.COM - Porcini Mushroom © Alessio Cola 171
FOTOLIA.COM - Ciaramicola dolce Pasquale umbro © claudio 172
FOTOLIA.COM - Corkscrew © Stefano Tiraboschi 172
FOTOLIA.COM - Panpepato © Marzia Giacobbe 173
FOTOLIA.COM - crocchette di patate © Alexandra 176
FOTOLIA.COM - Zwei größer Stück Käse vakuumiert © Daorson 176
Polenta Valdostana - Foto Marco Scataglini 177
FOTOLIA.COM - fontina italiana © Lsantilli 178
FOTOLIA.COM - Cabbage © Victoria Dolidovich 178
FOTOLIA.COM - Gewürz, Wacholder © Andre B. 179
FOTOLIA.COM - Purple Garlic © Tomboy2290 179
FOTOLIA.COM - Ramo di salvia © Studio Gi 179
FOTOLIA.COM - Ofenkäse © ExQuisine 180
FOTOLIA.COM - Uovo rotto © spinetta 180
FOTOLIA.COM - Leeks on a white background © iaroslava 181
Fricandò domo bianco - Foto Marco Scataglini 181
FOTOLIA.COM - Sardele in saòr - Antipasti di pesce del Veneto © Comugnero Silvana 184
FOTOLIA.COM - White Onion © Tomboy2290 185
FOTOLIA.COM - Panada - Primi piatti - Ricette tradizionali del Veneto © Comugnero Silvana 185
FOTOLIA.COM - rice © victoria p. 186
FOTOLIA.COM - Green pea © Vasilius 186
FOTOLIA.COM - sliced red onion © Jack Kunnen 187
FOTOLIA.COM - Erbe e spezie © francovolpato 187
FOTOLIA.COM - Butter curls © Viktor 187
FOTOLIA.COM - kalbsleber rohfleisch © Lucky Dragon 187
FOTOLIA.COM - baccalà alla vicentina © spinetta 188
FOTOLIA.COM - Salt and pepper shaker on a white background © Africa Studio 188
FOTOLIA.COM - Filetti di acciughe sott'olio © MarcoBagnoli Elflaco 189
FOTOLIA.COM - Pinto beans or mottled beans arranged in a frame © Lusoimages 189